Sports Parenting

W9-BXZ-476

"With practical advice, Jim and Janet show how to best parent a child in sports, eliminate the possible frustrations and disappointments, and bring out the best in a sports experience."

—DAVE DRAVECKY, PRESIDENT,
OUTREACH OF HOPE

"*How to Win at Sports Parenting* puts kids and sports into the proper context for success—personal success and family success."

—RICHARD SCHULTZ, EXECUTIVE DIRECTOR,
UNITED STATES OLYMPIC COMMITTEE

"I've known the Sundbergs for years. As a teammate and friend, I've seen Jim and Janet's children grow up in an environment of love, discipline, and support. Those threads weave their way through Jim and Janet's book. I highly recommend it for every family but especially those interested in or involved with sports."

—DON SUTTON, MAJOR LEAGUE
BASEBALL HALL OF FAME

"This is a must-read book for all parents and youth league coaches! The wisdom and practical insights the Sundbergs share make this a win-win situation for young people and their parents. It's past time for a book of this type that goes back to the basics, fundamentals, and enjoyment of sports."

—DAL SHEALY, PRESIDENT AND CEO,
FELLOWSHIP OF CHRISTIAN ATHLETES

"Sharing time with your children through sports is a wonderful thing. The Sundbergs give you the blueprint to help make the experience enjoyable for everyone."

—NANCY LIEBERMAN-CLINE, HEAD COACH AND
GENERAL MANAGER, DETROIT SHOCK–WNBA

"Jim and Janet's book is an outstanding resource for members of our Parents Association for Youth Sports (PAYS) Program. A great textbook for keeping things in perspective."

—FRED C. ENGH, PRESIDENT AND CEO,
NATIONAL ALLIANCE FOR YOUTH
SPORTS

"Play-by-play inspiration with practical advice and insight for parents who want their children to have fun while learning the disciplines and joy of sports."

—MARILYN OSHMAN, CHAIRMAN,
OSHMAN SPORTING GOODS

"Good reading for all parents with kids involved in sports. Must reading for parents who try to live their athletic dreams through their kids."

—ZIG ZIGLAR, AUTHOR,
MOTIVATIONAL TEACHER

"Essential reading for all families involved in sports! *How to Win at Sports Parenting* provides a great opportunity for parents and children alike to make their growing-up-with-sports experience a healthy and rewarding process."

—NORM MILLER, CHAIRMAN OF THE
BOARD, INTERSTATE BATTERIES

How to Win at
Sp⬤rts
Parenting

Maximizing the Sports
Experience for You and Your Child

Jim and Janet Sundberg

WATERBROOK
PRESS

HOW TO WIN AT SPORTS PARENTING
PUBLISHED BY WATERBROOK PRESS
5446 North Academy Boulevard, Suite 200
Colorado Springs, Colorado 80918
A division of Random House, Inc.

All scripture quotations, unless otherwise indicated, are taken from the *Holy Bible, New International Version* ®. NIV®. Copyright © 1973, 1978, 1984 by International Bible Society. Used by permission of Zondervan Publishing House. All rights reserved. Scripture quotations marked (NLT) are taken from the *Holy Bible, New Living Translation,* copyright © 1996. Used by permission of Tyndale House Publishers, Inc., Wheaton, Illinois 60189. Used by permission. All rights reserved.

The authors wish to give special thanks to Jim Nelson Black and Gary Wilde for their invaluable contribution in pulling together this material and coaching us through our first book.

ISBN 1-57856-354-2

Published in association with the literary agency of Alive Communications, Inc., 1465 Kelly Johnson Boulevard, Suite 320, Colorado Springs, Colorado 80920.

Library of Congress Cataloging-in-Publication Data
Sundberg, Jim.
   How to win at sports parenting : maximizing the sports experience for you and your child / Jim Sundberg.— 1st ed.
     p. cm.
   ISBN 1-57856-354-2
   1. Sports for children. 2. Parent and child. 3. Sports for children—Psychological aspects. I. Black, Jim Nelson. II. Title.

GV709.2 .S96 2000

                            99-059440

Printed in the United States of America
2000—First Edition

10 9 8 7 6 5 4 3 2 1

To our children: Aaron, Audra, and Briana.
You not only exemplify a variety of unique gifts and talents,
but you have God's empowering presence to be what He has called you to be
and to do what He has called you to do.
You are the greatest joy and blessing in our lives.
We are thankful for the privilege of being your parents.

And
to my father and mother,
who after fifty years of marriage are still committed to one another.
Thank you for all the things I don't have space to list!
Special thanks to my dad for his courage in letting me open our family's
home for all to see through this book.

Contents

Preface

You're committed to making your child's sports experience the best it can be. You're convinced that sports have something to offer, but you want to see for yourself and go about it the right way. Now you've decided to take a closer look.

Maybe you have an older child already participating. Or maybe your younger child is about to enter into sports, and you've seen something in his or her eyes that makes you think this would be a good fit. Even if your children excel in scholastic or artistic pursuits, you may have wondered if sports wouldn't expand their horizons and help them become even more accomplished and more self-confident. If so, congratulations! You're on the right track.

But for the sports experience to be everything you want it to be in your family, you'll need to plan your approach. And no matter how far along you are, it's never too late to start. A good plan will put you and your kids on the same page. It will help you communicate, show you the direction to go, and give you a road map to get you there. That's what this book is all about. Here's just a preview of the steps to a great family game plan you'll develop—

Step 1: Begin monitoring the level of sports tension in your family.

Step 2: Seriously plan for fun.

Step 3: Begin assessing the motivational makeup of your child(ren).

Step 4: Determine to focus on character development, win or lose.

Step 5: Check to make sure that the best life lessons are hitting home with your kids.

Step 6: Be sure you are getting your own needs met so you can best meet the needs of your child.

Step 7: Determine your basic game-day personality and work on turning its weaknesses into strengths.

Step 8: Don't assume; find out what your children actually want.

Step 9: Strive for the highest levels of communication in your family.

Step 10: In coach-conflict situations, first pull back so you can view things through the coach's eyes.

In the chapters to come, you'll plunge into these issues headlong. You'll find pertinent information, practical examples, and application exercises to help you navigate the sometimes choppy waters of youth sports. The goal is to gain more enjoyment from sports participation while laying a foundation for emotional well-being in your entire family.

With all the stresses our culture is undergoing today, it's more important than ever that we discover ways to live together peacefully. Sports allow families to enjoy one another and to come together as a more cohesive unit. There is tremendous value in that, even if your child never goes beyond the early school years in athletics.

Together, Janet and I have raised two children to adulthood—Aaron and Audra—both of whom are happily married and living in different parts of the country now. Our third child, Briana, is wrapping up her high-school career, and we're very pleased with how she's developing into a lovely, talented young lady. We proudly point to our kids as our best qualifications for writing this book.

Even now, as we watch Briana on the volleyball court, Janet and I believe that raising our kids with sports is one of the greatest, most enjoyable, and most successful things we've ever done. We've learned so much about ourselves and each other. We've experienced some terrific quality time and family bonding. And we know that the years with your child in sports can be the best years of your life too.

During the seasons I played and broadcast Major League Baseball, Janet was the principal sports parent in our household. Throughout this book, I rely on her experience from those days, as well as her educational background in psychology and human behavior. As you read, we hope you'll soon discover that fun and fear can't occupy the same space. Consequently, as you learn methods of reducing stress in your sports experience, you'll be replacing fears with fun for both you and your child. Now that's something to look forward to!

Finally, I want you to know that this book isn't just another exercise in motivational hype. We've included down-to-earth strategies for you to use on the field and at home. Nor is this book another collection of memoirs from a former jock; rather, it's an invitation to your whole family to build fulfilling memories that will last a lifetime.

Thanks for being open to change and willing to make a difference in your child's life. Janet and I hope you find this book helpful, fun, and informative. Now, let's play ball!

—Jim and Janet Sundberg

Notes to the Reader

USING THIS BOOK

The information in this book has a workbook aspect to it. You'll find various exercises to work through, along with Family Game Plans to fill in at the end of each chapter. Why not work through these exercises with your spouse and/or kids? As appropriate, take time to discuss the issues together. Make it a family experience of growth, right along with going to games together.

ENJOYING THE "EXTRAS"

Throughout the body of this text we've scattered numerous tidbits of useful information as sidebar items. Sometimes these items come from our own experience, and sometimes we've drawn from other sources and authorities to provide practical help. When the sidebars are footnoted, you can find the sources in the notes section. "Adapted from" means that we've changed the wording somewhat or condensed the information to fit into a reasonable space; naturally, we've still credited the source of the ideas. The icons below will alert you as to the kind of information you'll receive in each sidebar.

SPORTS TO LIFE

Here you'll find important life lessons for parents and families. They're often quotable quotes that keep the big picture in focus.

PARENTING POINTS

Tips and pointers help you overcome confusion as you parent your sports-oriented family. Read these words of wisdom when you need practical problem-solving methods.

CAUTION!

This feature asks you to stop and think. Slow down, reflect a moment, and consider whether you're still headed in the right direction. Words of warning will help you make any necessary adjustments.

SURVEY SAYS...

Don't just take our word for it! Here are the facts and figures offered by the experts. (Of course, Janet and I also conducted informal surveys in our own hometown. We think you'll enjoy hearing about other real-life family members.)

WORKING THE FAMILY GAME PLANS

At the end of each chapter, you're invited to make it all practical and applicable, step by step. Think about what you've read, jot down some notes, and then plan to take action!

READING THE MINICASES AND EXAMPLES

We've used stories and vignettes to illustrate our points throughout this book. In most cases these accounts involve fictional composites of people and situations we've observed in youth sports over the years. Real names have always been disguised.

Pursuing the Winning Sports Experience

I remember thinking as a child, *Wouldn't it be great to play in the World Series someday?* And more... *Wouldn't it be awesome to come up to bat with the bases loaded and get the game-winning hit?*

Well, my moment had actually come. Even though the possibility of the World Series was still a few pitches away, I could get there with one swing of the bat. I was the starting catcher for the Kansas City Royals in the seventh game of the American League play-offs. Our team had fought its way back from a three-game deficit to keep our play-off hopes alive. The winner of this seventh game would go on to the world championship.

And now I stood looking into the eyes of Toronto pitcher Dave Steib, with the bases jammed and a chance to make it all come true.

In many ways it was *already* a dream come true. Last game of the play-offs. Chance of a lifetime. A trip to the Series in the balance. And there I was, right in the middle of it.

But what would happen next? How would I respond to this life-changing opportunity?

As we begin the journey of this book, talking about all the things that parents and children can learn from the sports experience, I can't help making some important connections with my own background and all the things that led to my chance at long dreamed-for glory.

The key connection is this: *Pressure!*

Sports provides so many opportunities for social, emotional, and physical growth. The pressures, however, are enormous. They loom large at the professional level, of course. But parents, as you know, the pressures begin as soon as little Tommy dons his first pair of shin guards or little Susie first aims her toe at the heart of a soccer ball.

And every day the pressures are increasing for our youngsters in sports.

I'll get back to my game-winning opportunity in a moment, but first think with me a little more about how youth sports programs have changed over the years. Let's focus on that pressure, on the potential for parental guilt, and on how we're going to win at this whole new ball game—by choosing the best goals for our families.

FEEL THE PRESSURE?

I spent sixteen years of my life in Major League Baseball and another ten years teaching people about sports. After all that and after watching my three children participate in competitive sports during their growing-up years, I've come to understand just how difficult it can be to deal with all the emotions. I've often said that I now believe it was harder, emotionally, to watch my kids compete than it was for me to play in the World Series.

That incredible slice of reality led me to write this book. It was the pressure, not of pro sports, but of family life with young athletes that motivated me to start writing! And I'm quite sure you can relate. I'm quite certain that you've felt those pressures too.

You see, historically, youth sports programs began as a way to have fun, gain life skills, experience the benefits of physical fitness, and learn to compete in a team atmosphere. But mounting evidence of emotional and physical conflict on the playing fields in recent years has prompted many to ask, "What has gone wrong?" Even those responsible for much of the out-of-control behavior—including parents totally caught up in the whirlwind of activity—are beginning to ask, "What can we do to make this fun again?"

In his recent book, *Why Johnny Hates Sports,* Fred Engh, president of the National Alliance for Youth Sports, observed that the pressure to win at all costs is taking the fun out of the game for many people. Too many parents are applying professional standards to amateur sports, with the result that the level of expectation is ratcheted up to the unreasonable. What we're seeing is a highly charged atmosphere on the field and the court that has a direct impact, not just on the youngsters who play the games, but especially on coaches, referees, game organizers, and other officials.

> As an extreme example of how bad things can get in youth sports, the story of high school student Mike Cito and his father, Stephen, is difficult to beat. According to newspaper accounts of the incident, referees stopped a high school football game when they found that five players had been gashed during the game. They discovered Mike Cito's helmet contained a buckle that had been sharpened like a razor, causing the injuries to his opponents. One player had a wound that required twelve stitches.
>
> Mike, a junior, was kicked off his team and expelled from his school. His father, a dentist, stepped forward and admitted that he had sharpened the buckle because he was unhappy about the unfair treatment his son had received from referees in the previous week's game. What is going on when a father turns his son into a dangerous weapon because he is upset by a referee's decisions?[1]

All across the country, groups like the National Alliance for Youth Sports, the American Youth Soccer Organization, Pop Warner Football, and others are looking for ways to reduce these pressures. One way they've found is to come up with a code of conduct for parents, along with videos and handbooks on good sportsmanship. Some groups hold preseason training camps for parents, helping them learn appropriate behavior at youth events. "We all live through our kids," Engh says. "Therefore we do some very strange things."

While I'm pleased by the current explosion in the popularity of youth athletics, I'm troubled by the corresponding increase in aggression and unsportsmanlike conduct—not by the players, but by their parents! Ideally, sports should be wholesome and fun. However, I've seen an increase in demanding schedules, underappreciated coaches, and overzealous competitions that compromise the best efforts of well-meaning parents. These folks are often ill-equipped to balance the negative influences with the benefits youth sports can offer.

In all of my experience in the highly competitive sports culture, I've come to the realization that it's easier to keep my perspective by focusing on the big picture. The big picture in this book means keeping questions like these in the forefront of our thinking: How can you and I, as parents, increase the fun in our children's sports activities? How can we diffuse the fear of failure that haunts many of our kids? How can we eliminate the confusion between roles and expectations? And how can we relieve the tension so many of us feel as we drive up to the athletic complex? Those are the things we need to explore together.

DROP THAT GUILT!

Does it sound like I'm going to pile on the guilt? Give you 101 more things to do? Tell you to join a 12-step group for happy parenting? Well, don't worry. My intent isn't to overburden you, because I know that your schedule is already full just being a parent. Instead, I want to encourage you to explore a new approach to your child's sport, an approach that will help you respond more appropriately to tense situations and interact more responsibly with your child, her coach, and other parents and their kids.

Because of the intense emotions that run through sports, my wife and I believe that youth sports parents need to exercise an extra degree of caution. More so than parents of other kids. It's not a double standard but simply a recognition that sports can drive our passion and adrenaline to extreme levels. As a parent, I know that my emotional energy when my kids play could probably power the gymnasium lighting system. And I know I'm not alone in this. If you're a sports parent, you've felt like that too. We all need to equip ourselves to be more skilled at responding to the highs and lows of the sports experience.

If you can gain a better idea of what the big picture should be, then you'll be able to handle the specific difficulties your child's sports experience will bring. After all, what we learn on the playing field can teach us a lot about life and how to get the most out of it. But none of that happens by accident. For a child to get the most out of the sports experience, we parents should firmly understand that we do not need to be an expert in our child's sport or in her sports career. Wouldn't it be freeing to know that you don't have to stay on top of your kids to make sure they get everything right, all the time, in order for them to be successful?

That's just one more guilt trip you don't need to take!

My view is that sports can provide a great environment for mutual encouragement and support within the family. The sports scene produces many pockets of time where parents and their children can be together. The problem is that while boys and girls are out to have fun and enjoy the game at their own pace, their parents may have much loftier goals. Visions of high-school stardom, of winning an athletic scholarship, or of entering a professional career can produce parental expectations that are far beyond the child's ability to perform.

Then the child can start to feel guilty too. With all of this guilt and fear fogging up the home atmosphere, we sometimes see the development of an unhealthy codependency between parent and child. And as painful as this situation can be for the child, it can be even more stressful for parents, complicated by the fact that it's usually the parents who can't separate their emotions from those of their children. These are the situations that can lead to those embarrassing outbursts by parents at game time.

There is so much hope for a better way! The sports experience offers a great environment for families to grow closer in love and harmony. But there has to be a commitment to this greater good—and the patience to get there. That's not easy, because what comes naturally to us is not the best goal.

What do I mean? Well, I've had dads come up to me at our baseball camps and tell me that I needed to move their kid up a notch so he could "get the most out of the experience." I know what they mean by that, but I normally ask, "What do you want your child to get out of this camp? What do you really want to happen in these next five days?" Our coaches at the youth camps are not going to make any child into a Major League ballplayer, especially in a week! So what are these parents expecting? What do they want their child to accomplish?

Sometimes I can read the answer in their eyes: "My child is better than the rest of the kids his age, and I want you to recognize how much I've worked with him. I want you to know how much I know about his sport. I want you to recognize how good a parent I am." Far too often that's the underlying motivation for pushing kids beyond their ability to handle it. Parents who want to be "a good parent" sometimes try to use their child's skill and success to display their own parenting expertise. Even if their kid is an outstanding player, and even if he or she does have the talent to make it to the higher levels, putting that kind of pressure on a boy or girl at such an early age is not the best thing a parent can do.

So in this book we will talk about an intentional goal to have fun. We'll consider how to develop trust through a family's sports experience, and talk about how you can mindfully rework losing situations into something good. And yes, we will talk about the value of winning and keeping the motivation high. We'll ask, What does it mean to be a winner? What is victory, and how can I stop fearing defeat? And at what stage in a child's development should winning become an important part of the thinking and planning?

Of course we hope that our child may turn out to be successful on the field. The most important thing, though, is to grow the relationship between yourself and your child, establishing a framework of positive interaction. This relationship can help to instill courage, confidence, character, trust, and many other important personal traits as you go through things together. You are there to guide and to interpret what happened. You're there to reflect feelings, provide encouragement, and offer comfort. With a foundation like that, your kids will thrive in sports, regardless of playing time or wins and losses. They'll learn life skills that can contribute more than you'll ever know to their physical and emotional well-being. All these things, I'm sure, are your deepest desires for your children.

NOW, BACK TO THE GAME...

When I stepped into the batter's box on that autumn day in 1985, I remember thinking, *What am I going to do now?* I looked out at the mound and thought, *If I were Steib, pitching to Sundberg, I'd throw him a slider.* So I was thinking slider, and sure enough, he threw me a slider, but it was too low. I let it go. Ball one.

What happened next was the most incredible thing I could imagine, going against all the odds. Once again, I was looking for a slider, but for some reason, at the last moment, something looked different about the windup and delivery, and Steib threw me a fastball. It was up and out over the plate, but away from me...and I swung anyway.

Now that was totally opposite of anything I would normally do as a hitter. We're not trained to go for that pitch in that situation, but my reaction was instinctive and immediate. I got a pretty good piece of the ball, and it shot up high, down the line toward the right-field corner. The wind was blowing in that direction that night and for a second I thought it was going to be out of the park. But the ball just hung up there like it would never come down.

Did you ever have one of those dreams when you were a kid where giants were chasing you and you couldn't run away? Well, running the bases felt just like that. I was digging toward first base but I couldn't get my feet going fast enough, and everything seemed garbled. I was watching the ball going down toward the right-field corner in slow motion, and the right fielder was going after it, heading straight for the fence. The replay showed that he hit the wall and, as he hit it, the fence bowed out at the exact moment the ball came down. It landed right on top of the fence. If the fielder hadn't hit the fence so hard, the ball would have gone out of the park, in which case it would have been a grand-slam home run. Instead, it fell back inside the park, and I had to run the bases.

There was an incredible hush in the ballpark at that moment. The ball went so high, and everybody was guessing where it would fall, waiting with eyes glued to that tiny white dot. What an awesome moment to remember.

Today I can say that I enjoyed that experience more than any other in my baseball career. A grand slam would have been great, but I got a triple out of it, and that was enough, all we needed. It was the game winner, sending three runners across home plate. My only frustration was that as everybody on our team jumped up and down in the Royals dugout, celebrating the moment, I couldn't go over there and jump up and down with them. I was standing on third base, all by myself! The players were all going crazy, but there I was, reveling in the most comfortable loneliness I've ever known.

The Royals went on to win that game, which gave us the American League Pennant and a trip to the World Series. But I still remember that moment in the play-offs like it was destiny.

Destiny—that word should become an important reference point for us as we approach the higher levels of the sports experience with our kids. I've come to believe that for an athlete to make it to the pros, or even the Olympics, it is not going to be because that athlete's parents "willed it." Oh, we've heard those stories about the parent who put so much of his energy into his child's sport and did indeed reap great success. But at what price to the child? At what price to the family?

You can teach a kid the rules of the game, and you can do everything you know to get him or her prepared for the competition. But at some point they just have to do what they have to do. That's what I mean by destiny. It calls for parents and coaches to allow kids a good amount of freedom. Let them find out for themselves what works and what doesn't, so that in those critical moments they will have the courage to take a calculated risk, if that's what they're meant to do.

Parents never set out with the goal of making their child miserable. They never go into sports for that reason, but sometimes they lack the emotional skills to do it any other way. Without some source of balance or a framework for interpreting what happens on the field, the aggressive nature of the game can make us say and do things we might regret the rest of our lives. So how do we plan for that? When our daughter comes home crying because her team lost, or our son drops what could have been the winning touchdown, how should we respond? What can we do?

That's where I hope this book will be valuable to you. I hope it will help you, the parents who are so deeply affected by kids' sports pressures, to better navigate the rough waters of youthful competition. I hope you'll one day look back and see that through sports you've grown happier and healthier as a whole family.

Bottom line, I want you to know how to keep all this activity at your house, well, fun. Because that's when athletic competition truly becomes a winning sports experience.

PART ONE

The Family and Youth Sports

CHAPTER ONE

The Bad News: Pressured Kids and Tense Families

Tennis parents, the early stages.

et's begin by eavesdropping on a few families you may know...

On the long drive home, the Johnson family sat in silence. *Same old thing*, Juanita thought. *Another night of grumpy twins, Kevin trying to console them, and supper time ruined as usual.*

"Look, you girls did the best you could; it just wasn't your day."

"Yeah, right, Mom. Like giving up four goals in the first three minutes is really great soccer!"

Actually, the twins had done pretty well, but they weren't going to let it go. As the minivan pulled into the garage and everyone got out, Juanita suddenly felt how much she loved her two little redheads. Then she flinched as Jody unleashed a vicious kick into her equipment bag to send it into the corner.

"Hey! Cut it out!" yelled Kevin.

Cody started to cry again.

Why can't we win a game once in a while? Why? Juanita felt her face getting hot. *Dear God, I just want this family to be happy.*

———————

"Aw, c'mon, Freddy," said Jason. "You're not gonna fall or anything." Nine-year-old Freddy Ramirez hesitated, knowing this was the biggest day of his life. Starting pitcher in just a couple of hours! As Coach had handed him the game ball last night, Freddy remembered glancing over at his dad and feeling the warmth of his father's proud, smiling eyes.

But I really want to go rollerblading with Jason. "Just put on those wrist things and let's go," said Jason. Twenty minutes later, Freddy tearfully limped up the driveway holding his right arm. His elbow dripped blood onto his T-shirt, the swelling already kicking in.

"Dad! I got hurt! Daaad!"

Mr. Ramirez came out the front door, glanced at the blood, and said, "Oh, great! There goes today's game." The look he gave his little boy at that moment was anything but warm and proud.

———————

"What's to eat, Dad?"

"How'd you do at tryouts, Larnell?"

"Pretty good; made a sweet tackle. Anything to eat?"

"Did the coach see it?"

"I think so; I dunno."

"What do you mean, you don't know? Either he saw it or he didn't, right?"

"Well I think he did; I guess."

"Anybody get cut today?"

"A couple guys. Hey—nothing in the fridge!"

"How many are they going to keep, anyway?"

"I guess forty or so. Man, I'm hungry. What's this green stuff?"

"Well didn't Coach Kester say…"

Let it go, Dad, Larnell thought wearily. *I'm tired and hungry. I've got four hours of homework ahead of me and a chemistry quiz first thing in the morning. I haven't had more than five hours sleep any night this week, and I'm supposed to be getting A's and B's, right? Give me a break here!*

"You just don't care, do you, Larnell?"

"Huh?"

"You don't care, one way or the other. Scholarship, no scholarship."

"Yeah, I care."

"No, you don't. Not nearly enough. And you're gonna end up getting cut, too. And then don't come around blaming me, my man."

"Oh, I guess it's guacamole dip."

Recognize any of these kids? Any of the parents?

If you're a sports family, I'm sure you do. And no doubt your stories are also variations on the same theme: *The thrill of victory and the agony of defeat,* whether at the game or at home. Great highs and terrible lows. It's all there, making youth sports and its family connection something to love and often something to dread. Let me tell you how it's been with me…

MY STORY: KID OR ROBOT?

I grew up across the street from a ballpark, and by the time the sun came up in the morning I was already thinking about playing baseball. I was the kid who organized the sandlot games in our neighborhood. There were five or six of us who played most of the time, and they all knew that Jim Sundberg was the organizer. I called everybody up and got them out to play, and I laid out the diamonds each day.

You see, the ball field had been built for older kids, and that meant I had to set up shorter base paths and field markers so we could reach the fences with our power shots. I'd also decide what type of game we would play on any given day. I had a left-field diamond, a third-base diamond, a right-field diamond, or whatever we needed for a particular type of game. The idea was to keep the boundaries small enough so that, even as little kids, we could still hit home runs.

I had great fun organizing those games. I was outside playing all day long, practically every day during the summers, and I was completely saturated with baseball. My dad, a letter carrier, usually left the house early in the morning and arrived back home by midafternoon. He was even more excited about going out to play than I was, if that was possible. When he came home around 2:30, it wasn't, "Hi, Jim, how was your day?" It was, "Okay, son, grab your glove and let's go." It felt good knowing that my dad thought I was important enough to take up his time that way. I had his total attention, and there was nothing better.

But he coached me a good deal too.

Now, pressure from the team coach is one thing, but coaching pressure from Mom or Dad has an added dimension to it. After all, what we want from our parents far transcends mere skill improvement on a ball field. When all is said and done, we long to know that our parents love us with all their hearts—unconditionally—whether we hit the game-winning single or strike out, whether we field the grounder cleanly or end up with a bloody lip. And let's admit it: Most of us parents fall

SPORTS TO LIFE

NEVER GOOD ENOUGH?
Kevin Mitchell, on what Willie Mays said to him after a famous barehanded catch:
"I didn't teach you that. Catch the ball with your glove!" [1]

short of extending that kind of perfect acceptance to our little athletes. As well-meaning and as good-hearted as we are, we're all caught up with our own *performance* as adults; somehow that trickles down to the kids.

I remember one time in Little League when I'd played an outstanding game. I had hit three home runs that day, and I had one strikeout. After the game I went over to my dad and asked, "Well, what did you think of that?" His response was automatic: "Jim, if you had kept your elbow up like I showed you, you wouldn't have struck out."

Dad meant well. His intentions were good. He just figured he was helping me do my best by pushing a little harder. He loved me; he genuinely wanted to help.

Would it have been good for me to ask for a little more affirmation? No doubt. But a child just isn't ready to do that, is he? For me, growing up in a Swedish family in the Midwest, open communication of emotions, or any expression of our inner feelings, just wasn't encouraged. Mom and Dad were good parents, and they took good care of my brother, my sister, and me. But emotional reactions to the everyday stresses of life were held in check. It was this attitude, I believe, along with our family's intense focus on baseball (and on my athletic interests in particular), that made me sometimes feel more like a programmed robot than a real person.

I've discovered that growing up in family situations like that can lead to emotional problems later in life for kids who are wired in a certain way. Family members who aren't in touch with their feelings don't have a very high emotional IQ, or what I refer to as EQ. If they haven't learned to monitor their emotions or to read them in other people, then they're probably going to struggle with feelings of inadequacy or failure. They're going to cope poorly, and they're not going to be able to teach effective coping skills to their kids.

YOUR STORY: BAD NEWS IN THE FAMILY?

We need coping skills, because we react so intensely to sports. In our work with young people and parents, Janet and I have observed how readily sports involve and incite the emotions. Sports activities are stimulating and exciting, and they certainly should be fun. But they also demand an emotional response. So when tense moments arise, parents may explode, overreact, or respond negatively to their own children in more subtle, though no less destructive, ways. Then the good news of fun becomes the bad news of pressured kids and tense families.

The bright side, however, is that we parents can learn to understand our role and become real winners at sports parenting. As we apply some basic principles, we can promote happy and healthy sports experiences for our children. So right at the beginning, as you launch into this book, I'd like to suggest three foundational principles to keep in mind. They're practical "pressure checks," in the form of questions, that can signal you when the bad news is infecting your own family.

PRESSURE CHECK #1: ARE WINNING AND LOSING OVERSHADOWING RELATIONSHIP?

Parents of kids in sports need to stop and think about what really matters most in life. If you'll just stop and think, you'll be able to approach your children's involvement in sports with a much better attitude. The goal is to be able to say, without hesitation, "My child and I will be just fine whether or not we win this game."

> *You only have to bat 1.000 in two things—flying and heart transplants. Everything else you can go four for five.*
>
> —BEANO COOK

Whether he or she becomes a star athlete in high school, wins a scholarship for college, or has a shot at making the pros is not the biggest thing in your lives. The biggest thing is that your family is the team that should always come first. And if you really care about what matters in life, you'll be able to celebrate every game and every day, win or lose. In other words, what you're doing as a family is so much more important than a ball game.

Does your child have to win every sporting event for you to feel like a winner? Or do you have the courage to let go of your own driving need to win, simply accepting your children for who they are? I came across the words of a mother, a writer working at home, who discovered just how precious it is to pay attention to the parent-child relationship over less important matters—like work:

> One day, when Ariel was three and I was at my desk working hard, she sat at my feet in deep concentration. One by one she removed the long punched-hole edges of computer paper that I had thrown in the wastebasket, and bit by bit she stuffed them into a red sock. It was a large sock, and it took her small hands a long time to fill it.
>
> Since that time I've never been able to part with that sock. I look back at that scene, and this is what I see: a mother, frantic under deadline, sits hunched at her desk. At her feet is her daughter, linking her mother to another world. In this world there are no deadlines. Work is play, and there's all the time in the world to do it.[2]

Yes, winning and losing are a part of life. But children start out being into sports for the "play." In some ways, it's a whole different world for them. If we approach their games with the grim determination we bring to our work, then losing becomes the ultimate failure. It all starts to become work for everybody at home. When we refocus on our relationships, though, our families can remain happy and healthy through it all.

Why not pay a little more attention to the interactions among you? You'll discover great potential for fulfillment and satisfaction beyond the box scores! Add to the warmth however you can; keep the love flowing, win or lose.

When the tranquilizer finally took effect, Johnson
was dragged off the field and the relief pitcher
safely assumed the mound.

PRESSURE CHECK #2: IS THE "DREAM" COMING

ONLY FROM MOM OR DAD?

As a kid, I had great times practicing and playing ball with my dad. But I felt that those times were for him, too. It was his chance to be engaged in something he had missed growing up. Dad was a frustrated athlete, in part because his own father, busy with overtime shifts during the war, had little time for sports. My grandfather would come home exhausted and spend the evening resting up for the next day of work. Since Grandpa had little spare time left over for his son's activities, my dad spent practically all *his* free time working with me.

But would I be able to fulfill my dad's dream of sports success? The question reminds me of a sad piece of dialogue spoken by Kevin Kostner in the role of Ray Kinsella in the film *Field of Dreams.* When asked, "What happened to your father?" he responded:

> He never made it as a ballplayer, so he tried to get his son to make it
> for him. By the time I was ten, playing baseball got to be like eating

YOUTH SPORTS DROPOUTS

A huge number of children stop playing sports after displaying initial interest. In a comprehensive survey of 1,183 athletes aged 11 to 18 and of parents of 418 athletes aged 6 to 10, researchers found that 35 percent of the young athletes planned to stop playing the next year. Nearly half the parents reported that their child was not interested in the sport anymore.

In a survey of 5,800 children who had recently stopped playing a sport. Their top 5 reasons for stopping were:

- I lost interest.
- I wasn't having fun.
- It took too much time.
- The coach was a poor teacher.
- There was too much pressure.[3]

vegetables or taking out the garbage. So when I was fourteen, I started to refuse. Can you believe that? An American boy refusing to have a catch with his father? Anyway, when I was seventeen, I packed my things, said something awful, and left.

Parents need not have "failed" in order to produce a similar family dynamic. I suspect the same sorts of tension will be felt in any family where the parents have achieved success and recognition in their field. But kids always perform best when they are free to enjoy their interests simply for the fun of it and not to meet the standards of their parents. For them, it's not the pressures, not the demand to excel, but just the idea that if I participate in this activity I can have a lot of fun, and I can do some things that I'll remember for the rest of my life. That's the motivation for a lot of the kids who are doing well in sports today. It's not that the extroverted parents blatantly said, "You have to do this!" It's not that the quieter, introverted parents conveyed the subtle message, "Please help us feel better about ourselves." No, it's that the child felt the freedom to do it just for the fun of it.

I know from my own relationship with my dad that parents who put a lot of pressure on their kids about sports or academics, or any other endeavor, run the risk of driving a wedge between themselves and their kids that may never be removed. It's no fun when a parent is always uptight, always applying more pressure, whether consciously or below the surface with a look, an offhand comment, or an overall attitude of anxiety. I often say this to parents in seminars: "If you put that kind of pressure on your kids, then you may as well prepare yourself for the fact that you will lose them one day. Because what you're actually doing is driving a wedge between yourself and your child." Many times they won't want to come back home once they've left the nest. Those kinds of pressures are hard to forget.

I know none of this is easy. Having attempted these things myself, I'm now experiencing a cultural boomerang. My dad spent so much time with me that I decided I wouldn't push my son so much. And what Aaron sensed (wouldn't you know it?) was that maybe I didn't care!

SURVEY SAYS

OLYMPIC ATHLETES TALK ABOUT MOM
AND DAD'S INVOLVEMENT
Of the fourteen women polled from the U.S. softball team,
- nine said both their parents were involved in their sports activities.
- one said neither was.
- ten said no one in their immediate family had any expertise in their sport.
- all fourteen said that the role of parents should be as supporters and encouragers, while the role of the coach should be as teacher and instructor.

This should be a relief to those parents who think they have to be everything to their child![4]

The truth is, I knew he was feeling the pressure anyway. Well-meaning family members and friends would sometimes say things like, "So, Aaron, are you going to be a big leaguer like your father?" Or, "Are you as good a ballplayer as your dad?" They were just kidding around, of course. But comments like that go straight to a child's heart, because he or she already worries about living up to parental expectations. I think the hardest thing for children to do is to go into the same profession as a parent, because on top of the pressures the world puts on them, they also have to battle their own insecurity. It's often easier for them to blaze their own trail and head in a different direction. Will we let them?

PRESSURE CHECK #3: HAVE THE PARENTS LEARNED TO LET GO?
We need to enjoy the freedom in the parent-child relationship. That is, freedom for the child to be what he or she really is, but also freedom for the parent who can say, "You know, it doesn't all depend on me." It's not how hard we push that will make our children successful or unsuccessful in life. It should give us a tremendous sense of freedom to be able to say, "I need to love my child, encourage my child, and discipline my child when she needs it—but wow!—it's not all up to me." The point is, there's a magic that's going to happen in your child's life, whether or not you're even there. As the old proverb says: "More things grow in the garden than the gardener sows." It's true, isn't it?

Our anxiety as parents seems to come out the strongest with first children. We wake up one day and realize we're parents; suddenly we've got this little tyke who's totally dependent on us, and we say, "Oh, Lord, what am I going to do with this child? It all depends on me!" Yet a friend of mine recently told me how fortunate he felt that his first child turned out to be a beautiful, talented, self-motivated little girl who let it be known very early in her life that there wasn't a lot her parents could do for her. "It took me about five minutes to realize that there was no way I was going to have much influence on what she would become or where she would go in life," he said with a grin. "She had such a strong sense of her own identity, and she was her own little person from the first day we brought her home."

Now and then we see a child like that who's just naturally secure and self-directed. That child could probably teach Mom and Dad a lot about their parental roles. But more often we think we've got this little lump of clay, and it's our job to shape and mold it. In reality, that clay has a natural shape and purpose designed into it from the start.

So listen, parents: *Relax!*

You can't control the other parents at your son's soccer match. You can't control the coaches on your daughter's volleyball team. You can't make the fans behave themselves at a swim meet or a basketball tournament. You certainly can't play the game for your child. You can observe and interpret what's taking place on the field, and sometimes you may get caught up in the sideshow, with matching T-shirts or war chants or whatever. But none of that has much connection with what's actually happening on the field. That part is beyond your control.

Yes, we have a key role to play in the maturity and development of our children, but we are not the ones who are supposed to make them successful in life. We just don't have that much power. So, Mom, Dad, let go a little bit!

PARENTING POINT

LASTING LIFE LESSONS FOR YOUR CHILD

Here's how to teach your child winning attitudes about sports. Be sure they hear things like this coming from you regularly:

- "You and I will be just fine whether or not we win this game."
- "You and I may have dreams and goals that differ; those that spring from your heart are beautiful and worthy in my eyes."
- "You and I can relax into the fun of sports. Let's be thankful for the miracle of muscles, sweat, blue sky, grass, a pumping heart, and sunshine. Isn't physical fitness great?"

Your child comes packaged with a natural design built in by the Creator. Your job, inasmuch as you're able, is to help your children recognize their own design and calling and then let them develop it.

It's ironic that so many parents say they believe their child is "unique," and then they turn right around and spend the rest of their lives trying to mold that child into something they think he should be. We decide that our plans, our visions for the future are too important to let go. In fact, *everything* has become so terribly important for us...

> *Our society has inundated us with the importance of importance.*
> *We have been conditioned to believe in the big, the fast, the expensive,*
> *and the far away. I'm still convinced that if you have to move even ten*
> *inches from where you are now in order to be happy, you never will be.*
> *Life becomes precious and more special to us when we look*
> *for the little everyday miracles and get excited again*
> *about the privilege of simply being human.[5]*
>
> —TIM HANSEL

Your child is a precious human being, much more than a number on a lineup card. And your child is here now, just as she is, needing you. One of your primary responsibilities at any sports event is simply to be there for him or her. Everything else—all your worries, your fears, your anxious plans for the future—all of that you can simply... *let go.*

Rather than working longer and harder to make our children successful, we parents can make a conscious decision about our dreams for them: "I'll be okay if I do not have this." Then, paradoxically, the future can shine even brighter than we ever imagined.

So what's keeping you from this approach? You may think, *I can't go forward unless my child wins a scholarship to the university.* That's silly! Of course you can. There are a lot of colleges and a lot of scholarships if you're willing to make some adjustments in your thinking. Maybe your child can start out in a less competitive program and transfer later. But what if he doesn't get a scholarship at all? You can still say, "I'd prefer for him to get the scholarship, but if not, we will work it out somehow." This attitude recognizes that there are always more options to consider.

Sometimes it's as if we don't have enough confidence in ourselves to believe that we actually have other alternatives. If that's your situation, you might find it helpful to sit down and think about your options with someone who knows the variety of opportunities that you can't see at the moment.

A FATHER-SON STORY: TOUGH START, HAPPY ENDING

I can't think of a better illustration of the narrowing of opportunities in a child's life than the story of former big-leaguer Jimmy Piersall. His early years with his dad were portrayed in the 1956 film *Fear Strikes Out,* starring Anthony Perkins and Karl Malden.

Have you seen it? What family devastation when winning is everything, when the dream comes only from Dad, when a son just can't do enough! In the film, Jimmy's mother becomes concerned as she watches her little boy practice sliding, over and over again, in a patch of dirt behind the house:

> Mom: Jimmy always looks so serious when he plays.
> Dad: He's a good boy; he tries hard.
> Mom: Too hard, sometimes.
> Dad: Nothing comes easy, and you know it; if he'll work hard enough, he could become a great ballplayer.
> Mom: Just like his dad; you were the best I ever saw...
> Dad: Playing for a factory team? Making a few dollars in my spare time? Oh no, what I'm thinking about is the big leagues. The Boston Red Sox. That's where Jimmy's going.

Later, when Jimmy's high-school team wins the state championship, with Jimmy making a game-winning throw from left field, Dad follows him into the locker room:

> Jimmy: We made it, huh?
>
> Dad: Yeah, you made it…with *luck* you made it. It was a good enough game for high school, but you weren't on your toes all the time, and you know it.

Jimmy's dad goes on to give a blow-by-blow critique, pointing out the many problems with his son's play. Afterward, Jimmy goes to the first-aid box for some aspirin. He's a sensitive young man.

After a brief stint in the minors, Jimmy does, indeed, make the Red Sox —only to be told that he'll have to play shortstop instead of the outfield. The years of pressure to perform have taken a toll on his nerves, and this change in direction throws him into a tailspin. Dad has taught him how to play outfield; it's what he knows, and he can't face the thought of doing things any differently. His sensitive nature, combined with all the stress, cause him to break down completely. Later, while talking with a psychiatrist, Jimmy still refuses to face the unhealthy relationship with his dad:

> Now look, Doc. Let me tell you something. I love my dad; he's the biggest thing in my life. He taught me and he straightened me out and he kept me in line. If it hadn't been for him standing behind me and pushing and driving me, *I wouldn't be where I am today!*

Where was Jimmy at that moment? Confined to a mental hospital.

But parents, this excellent movie—please rent it!—has a happy ending. Jimmy gained the courage to confront his dad. And Dad began to see that pure, unconditional love for his son mattered more than anything else. Jimmy Piersall went on to play big-league baseball for seventeen seasons—*because he wanted to do it.*

Parents like Jimmy's dad, like my parents and no doubt like yours, are the most love-filled in the world. They're like us, too, because they've worried about their children, they've worked hard for them, dreamed dreams for them. Every intention sprang from love; every motive flowed from a worthy vision of success.

But making children successful is not the same as helping them to know—to feel within their souls—how deeply they are loved. The good news is, we can do that and they'll be all right.

They really will be all right.

DEVELOPING THE FAMILY GAME PLAN

STEP 1: BEGIN MONITORING THE LEVEL OF SPORTS TENSION IN YOUR FAMILY.

Think back to the last time your child lost a game. Jot down your recollection of some of the words, attitudes, and actions of family members that evening:

What was positive about the experience?

How would you like the atmosphere to be different next time?

What things could you do to make that happen?

How well can you articulate your child's own dreams and goals for sports involvement? Write some of your hunches below. Then go check it out with your child.

Think about your dreams for your children in sports. If you seem to be pushing your own dreams instead of theirs, what first step can you take to begin letting go? Write your idea here:

CHAPTER TWO

The Good News:
Fun, Part I

(WHEN THE ADULTS ARE HEROES)

"Please go back to your seat, Mrs. Canfield. You
don't see any of the other parents blocking for
their kids, do you?"

I n 1987, toward the end of my career, I had the opportunity to play
for those lovable Cubbies in Chicago. We were playing an in-season
exhibition game against the southsiders, the White Sox, as the two
teams do every year. They call it the Windy City Classic, and usually only
the nonregulars see action in this game. However, manager Don Zimmer
apparently decided I might enjoy playing, so he put me in at third base.

Third base! I was a catcher. I had never played third base before, and I
was certain I'd embarrass myself by taking a bad hop in the mouth or letting

one of those evasive "worm burners" scoot between my legs. An infielder is supposed to be saying to himself, "Hit the ball to me." My secret prayer was "Hit the ball to short."

The most amazing thing happened, though, as I played the first eleven innings of that extra-innings game at third: not a single grounder came to me. Oh, you should have seen me diving to my right and diving to my left; however, because of my poor range, I just couldn't get to the ball.

All that diving looked pretty good, though. And no errors!

Anyway…the last three innings of this game were filled with craziness. We had run out of pitchers, and they needed someone to throw. Yes, you guessed it: yours truly. Star third baseman turned pitcher.

Over the last three innings I dueled it out with Steve Lyons, a first baseman—and we both held our opponents scoreless! I made the last out of the game in the bottom of the fourteenth by hitting a ball that the center fielder jumped into the ivy to catch. They stopped the game after that because we had to catch a flight. But Rick Sutcliff, one of the Cub pitchers, had already made me the MVP by putting a collection of Gatorade cups together as a trophy. What an exciting, tiring, scary, adventurous, thrilling, awkward, and satisfying day it was—and some of the most fun I ever had.

Actually, when I found out I was playing third base, I intentionally made it my goal to have as much fun as I could with the day. I didn't have a well-honed action plan or an elaborate set of strategies to put into play. Rather, I simply approached the game with a single-minded purpose: fun. It turned into an outstanding day of effective personal performance.

Here's the point of the whole story: If it's possible for a veteran big-leaguer to have fun at a ball game, wouldn't it be okay for little Tommy in Hometown Hockey, or young Susie in the River City Soccer Club to pursue the same thing?

Please don't misunderstand. Going for the fun is not a lackadaisical pursuit. I constantly tell parents, "You cannot *passively* pursue the fun in a sport;

you *plan* to do it!" How? I suggest that accomplishing real fun in youth sports requires at least two things: (1) a certain kind of involvement from the adults, and (2) some specific qualities of motivation within the kids. In this chapter, let's look at that first point. Then in the next chapter, we'll consider what a motivated child looks like.

INVOLVED AS HEROES

Key word: *involved.* Kids have fun in sports when their parents are involved. Not just any kind of involvement will do, however. You might call it by any number of names, but I like to think of this special kind of "being there" as *heroic.* That's right, the coaches, parents, and fans have determined to be heroes for their young people in the world of youth sports.

What a contrast to the general trend in our society today! Just think with me for a moment about a rather startling set of statistics, and you'll see what I mean. Here's what a recent national survey discovered about kids and their television sets:

- 53 percent of American children have televisions in their bedrooms (including 65 percent of 8- to 18-year-olds).
- 32 percent of kids ages 2 to 7 have in-room sets.
- 25 percent of 2 to 4-year-olds have in-room TVs.[1]

These kids spend an average of six hours daily, seven days a week—roughly the equivalent of an adult workweek—being influenced, taught, and manipulated by the "boob tube." Who are their heroes?

> Americans are living in a post-heroic age.... Defining "hero" as anyone with admirable courage (other than family or biblical figures), a study [by Scripps Howard News Service and Ohio University] revealed that the last 30 or 40 years has been a time of extreme cynicism toward heroes, in which a media-wise culture has witnessed the debunking and demythologizing of one so-called hero after another.

It's not a healthy trend, according to former U.S. Education Secretary William Bennett, author of the best-seller *The Book of Virtues:* "It is particularly important for young people to have heroes. This is a way to teach them by moral example, so that we can point to someone as an ideal."[2]

But I want to commend you, dear sports family. Your children are out there playing! They're using their muscles, interacting with others. They're not watching TV so much as drinking in the influence of all the adults around them on the fields, in the stands, at the dinner table. Great!

So you're involved, but *what kind of involvement is it?* Parents, coaches, fans—are you functioning as heroes for your kids?

NBA Co-Rookie of the Year [1995], Jason Kidd, says his heroes are his mother and father, who taught him the virtues of hard work and patience. Such talk may seem clichéd, but Kidd appears the living embodiment of it.

"When I was a boy, my father used to take me bowling," he says, "and I wasn't very good." But I always made excuses why I wasn't good. My father said, 'Quit that. The reason you're not a good bowler is that you don't practice.' And he was right. Now if I have a defect, I work at it. I don't make excuses."[3]

Jason said those things in 1996. He's had a lot of fun since then.

SERIOUSLY PURSUING FUN

We've already dealt with some of the saboteurs to fun, those destructive mechanisms that put undue pressure on kids and parents alike: Overzealous parents, for instance, whose own personal goals put unrealistic demands on their kids. Or parents whose children have become extensions of parental identities so the adults can now make another pass at becoming "stars" themselves. But this chapter is about the good news, about how kids can have fun because the adults are doing things right. What are their heroes like? What are they doing to make it fun? Consider four characteristics:

1. THEIR HEROES PRACTICE CONSISTENCY AND RELIABILITY.

This quality in adults produces self-discipline, consistent performance, and a sense of security in youngsters. If you don't believe it, just think about the child who's confused, anxious, and frustrated on the playing field and elsewhere.

There's young Bobby, for instance, a big thirteen-year-old with excellent baseball skills, who played in a competitive league. He worked hard at hitting but had an unusual habit: He would always slow down just a little bit as he ran to first base after making contact. No matter how hard the coaches worked with him to "run *through* the bag," he would—apparently unconsciously—put on the brakes just before the base and often be called out by a split second.

His father hollered. The coaches questioned.

But something inside Bobby seemed to be saying, "I just can't make it." He'd throw off his helmet, stomp his feet back to the dugout, but his big brown eyes conveyed a sense of hurt. The overwhelming feeling virtually dripping from his uniform was…*discouragement.*

And what was happening at home? Ron and Krystal were usually sitting on opposite sides of the bleachers, having separated for a time "to cool down" after a year of fighting. Ron had once played a year of single-A professional ball, so he knew the game and had taught Bobby a lot. But Krystal felt baseball had become everything to the family, that Ron, who also coached girls softball and helped with the high school JV, was never home because of all the game schedules.

Poor Bobby. He wanted, even more than base hits, to see his parents together. He wanted them consistently encouraging him, reliably at peace in

HOW TO APPROACH SPORTS AT TWO LEVELS

*Sports for the
Beginner Athlete*
Early sports are for exposure, expression, and fun, and that is how it should remain until age thirteen or so. From approximately age six to thirteen, children should not be involved in high-stress situations. Your responsibilities include:
- selecting open and flexible programs
- choosing leagues that play everybody
- monitoring the play and environment for safety

*Sports After
Age Fourteen*
Now it's time for the children to begin deciding how long or to what end they will pursue a sport. Your role is to:
- restrain from managing the child's athletic participation
- be there to support and encourage
- realize they're ready to work a little harder
- let them confront the importance of training and self-discipline

the home. Of course, it's not just the on-the-verge-of-a-breakup couple that exudes inconsistency. It comes through any time:
- coaches announce the starting lineup on Friday evening and then make major, last-minute changes on Saturday morning
- a dad brings his little girl to practice late—but sometimes on time—and sometimes not at all
- fans shout encouragement when the team is winning but hurl sarcasm when the team is down
- league or club officers call for volunteers and then handpick only the people they want for projects
- a mom always hugs her boy after a game—a winning game, that is, unless he's missed several free throws

You can be a strict parent; you can be quite permissive. But you simply must be consistent. If a child knows what to expect, day in and day out, he or she can thrive. But when the rules are constantly changing, when responses are thoroughly unpredictable, the kids have entered the realm of what mental health counselors call "crazy-making behavior." Nothing could be worse for a child hoping to grow in self-confidence.

2. THEIR HEROES TEACH LIFE LESSONS ON AND OFF THE FIELD.

We'll get specific about what the lessons are in chapter 5. But for now, simply realize that kids have fun in sports when they're *learning* from sports—learning important things that they can use for the rest of their lives. Be assured that teaching and learning is taking place, always. So the challenge is to make sure that what is being conveyed is intentional and worthy.

> *My father was a wonderful man.*
> *He was a very poor man and he'd never complain about nothing,*
> *but he was rich when it came to love. He used to wear long boots,*
> *and every night when he came home from work, one of us*
> *would have to take his boots off, one would bring hot water*
> *and the soap, and we would wash his feet.*
> *Then my sister would take a razor blade and cut his corns.*
> *When a man can have his kids do that, he is a very wealthy man.*
>
> —CHI CHI RODRIGUEZ, PRO GOLFER[4]

Chi Chi surely learned at least one important lesson from his father: Riches are nothing compared to love. That kind of life lesson is worthy to teach, whether in word or deed. We'll talk more in the next chapter about the lessons that can come from athletic involvement itself. But here I just want to stress that *children do as we do, not as we say.* Do they see us living the lessons we speak? The little learners are watching. They want to see the heroism in us. They want to have that kind of fun.

3. THEIR HEROES CONSTANTLY MODEL SPORTSMANSHIP AND ETHICAL CONDUCT.

I'll make this section brief because I think it's self-explanatory. But I've been encouraged to know that some of the world's greatest athletes and coaches have seen the value of living as role models for young people. Here are three who made their comments on ESPN:

> *I would like people not to think in terms of the 755 home runs I hit but think in terms of what I've accomplished off the field and some of the things I stood for.*
>
> —HANK AARON[5]

> *I have tried to follow in his footsteps and be as successful a human being as he has been. The basketball is a given, but the stuff that surrounds it, that's a lot more important, and I see that now. Coach Wooden would not have had his success if he didn't have his own moral and ethical background and his own integrity.*
>
> —KAREEM ABDUL-JABBAR[6]

> *The role model starts at home. It's Dad and it's Mom, and if Dad and Mom aren't there, you look for outside people. If there is something in my life that I have done in the way I carry myself that can help other people, go for it. It's there, it's an open book, I don't have a patent on it.*
>
> —WALTER PAYTON[7]

We parents and coaches in youth sports can hardly model heroism when winning becomes more important to us than fair play. Or when a competitive spirit draws us into questionable practices. That's when the fun fades away.

4. THEIR HEROES ENCOURAGE SOCIAL INTERACTION
AS A NURTURING BACKGROUND.

What makes for a winning sports experience that is truly fun? One high-school football coach in central Florida believes it's "a team that is tight"—parents included.

Coach Greg Register had a dismal season in 1998 (3-7). Adding to the disappointment was the fact that his team should have been awesome. They were fielding several scholarship-bound players, and most positions were loaded with talent.

But things never really gelled. In addition, the kids didn't seem to like one another very much. It was an almost daily occurrence to have little spats at practice, with name calling after hard hits. Bitter brawls would break out between the offense and defense. A spirit of one-upsmanship and put-downs seemed to prevail.

All of this prompted Register to make a rather daring announcement in the local papers at the beginning of the 1999 season. When asked to give a preview of strategies and prospects for the year, the other schools' coaches told of their plans to stress more discipline, practice longer and harder, implement new offensive or defensive systems. In contrast, Register said he would focus only on two things: increasing the teamwork and bringing the fun back to the game.

He admitted that he'd graduated numerous talented seniors and that prospects were dim for a team that had lost so many games during the previous year. Nevertheless, he realized that he'd been in football from the beginning for the joy of it—the fun of well-executed plays, the thrill of good, hard contact, and the bond of close camaraderie. He was determined, win or lose, that his players would know the fun of football too.

During the summer, he scheduled a team campout instead of extra practices. The team members were encouraged to become friends, and they did. They began hanging around with each other after school. They were in each other's homes doing homework, often sleeping over if the hours got too late. Imagine—kids of different racial backgrounds camping out together on somebody's family room carpet, then going to the beach on Saturdays, talking, enjoying the fellowship, growing in affection.

As for the parents, they were there. They planned tailgate parties and organized cookouts, breakfasts, and pregame meals. In the midst of this constant encouragement of the kids, win or lose, the parents got to know each other, too.

The most beautiful thing is that a lot of mentoring began taking place between fathers and other fathers' sons. Mothers were serving breakfasts to other mothers' boys. The kids knew they were being mentored and monitored by a whole community of adults who cared deeply for them. There were no fights and no delinquency, because these players knew they were being "watched"—*watched over,* that is.

And it all contributed to the fun of winning. The team started out with three early losses, and then kept winning to go 8-3 for the season. As I write this the Oviedo Lions are entering the quarterfinals of the 6A state play-offs and confidently aiming for the championship game in "The Swamp" at the University of Florida.

The point: When you are asked to play hard, to give it everything you've got on the goal line in the final minutes, you do it not merely because the coach wants it. You do it because you just can't bear to disappoint your best friends.

The team plays *as a team;* the team is having fun.

Remember: Fun teams are "tight"—including the parents. Fun teams have nurturing social interactions operating in the background. Work on setting up this kind of dynamic, and you'll be a hero to your young athletes.

STARTING EARLY, WIDENING THE EXPOSURE

It's best to put the emphasis on fun in sports—and in all your child's endeavors—right from the beginning. Let kids be kids! Let them be free to choose their forms of expression, and leave things open for them to explore all of their interests.

From the time our son was four years old he would say, "Daddy, I want to be just like you." As Aaron was growing up, I realized that he loved playing ball with me. He was athletically adept, but that deeper interest in sports didn't seem to be there. It's true that he eventually played on the varsity team in high school and was a scholarship pitcher in college. But during his sophomore year at Auburn University he decided that baseball wasn't really what he wanted to do in life, so he dropped out of sports.

Janet and I had sensed the pressure he was feeling in high school and college, and we could see that he was becoming more self-conscious about playing the game. Part of it was cultural, I suspect, because of the sense of expectation he felt. Or it may have been that the expectations he saw around him were just too high.

Whatever it was, we see now that we didn't have the perspective to introduce him into a lot of other things during those years. During his last couple of years in high school we talked about sports and what sort of major he might want to pursue, but it wasn't until midway through college, when he gave up sports, that we really connected with what Aaron wanted to do with his life. At that point we suddenly began thinking about what sort of transition he could make to find what would be the best fit for him. Of course, this brought home a lesson that we have since incorporated into everything we teach: Encourage early exploration and leave plenty of room for expansion.

Those early years are such formative years, and it's so important that you take advantage of that time to discover where your child's giftedness lies. Your children will be so much happier if you can make that discovery early and help them to build on it. Your kids can still capture it in their twenties, and I suspect that a lot of twenty- and thirty-year-olds are trying to do that in this country today. But how much better it would be if you could start sooner and give them a head start.

Someone has said that childhood is what you spend the rest of your life trying to get over. I don't think it has to be that way. If parents would spend a little time thinking about it when their children are still young and in their formative years, and when the child is still open to parental influence (which is before the age of thirteen), they would begin to discover the skills and interests that really propel their children. These will become their future careers and hobbies.

The point is, you may have a star pro athlete in your kitchen right now, eating her Cheerios with chocolate milk. (Go ahead, Dad, give her a nice smile!) Or you may have a very good computer programmer, a brilliant attorney, an inspiring professor, or a struggling artist. How will you know what's going to blossom in your child unless he or she is allowed to bloom?

DEVELOPING THE FAMILY GAME PLAN

STEP 2: SERIOUSLY PLAN FOR FUN.

What is your definition of "fun" in sports? Write it here:

What would you guess is your child's definition? Jot down your thoughts:

Check your guess with your child(ren), and talk about this issue together. Then consider what steps you could take to adjust your attitudes and actions to better meet your child's expectations for fun.

Idea:

Idea:

Idea:

Idea:

CHAPTER THREE

More Good News: Fun, Part II

(WHEN THE KIDS ARE MOTIVATED)

Embarrassing moments with 2-year-olds.

I just can't seem to get little Harvey going," said Mrs. Thompson. "He comes home from school, heads to the refrigerator for a snack, then camps out in the family room for the rest of the afternoon."

She went on to describe a regular ritual. As time for the Little League game approached, she'd roam through the house hunting up Harvey's "tools of battle": the glove, the bat, the uniform pieces, the shoes and socks and hat... "Did I mention the shoes?" Piled at the door, these accoutrements of ballpark war, of the impending clash of T-ball titans, would always be ready in time.

Unfortunately, by this time the little warrior was usually asleep.

"Is it me or is Harvey a tad undermotivated?"

Let's just say that some of us have less "ya gotta wanna" than others.

Yet we all need motivation. It gets us up in the morning and causes us to stretch ourselves toward accomplishment. It's important for people to be

PARENTING POINT

HOW ARE YOUR CHILDREN MOTIVATED?

Observe how your children interpret and react to the world around them so you can discover how they're motivated. Here are some clues you can watch for:

Motivated by Competition?

Do they initiate their own involvement because they love getting awards? Do you hear them talk a lot about winning or about who won a particular event? Once Briana came home discouraged because she didn't win an award for selling the most wrapping paper for a fundraiser. It turns out she came in second, but she still wasn't number one—the only prize awarded! Also, note whether your child talks about winning in the context of an *individual* endeavor or as a *team* effort.

Motivated by Relationships?

Does your child come more alive as more people gather around? If you had a number of people over to your home, which of your children would join in and who would slip away to her room?

If we sent our three kinds into our neighborhood, one child would come home with maybe one friend. Another of our kids would come home with a couple of friends. Yet another of our kids would call from someone's house, where they were hosting a block party with dozens of friends—plus all their dogs and cats! As a parent, you should already motivated, especially in companies and other organizations where they're working toward common goals. So a child who seemingly has no motivation at all will need to gain some gumption somewhere along the way. How to help him?

First learn to understand him, figure out how he's put together inside. In this regard, Janet and I have found the concept of "push or pull" to be especially helpful.

PARENTING POINT

HOW ARE YOUR CHILDREN MOTIVATED? (cont.)

have a good idea about how your child interacts socially, and that gives you good clues as to how they approach sports. Some kids are on the team mainly because of the friendships. Let them enjoy that!

Motivated by Challenges?

Does your child become energized when faced with an obstacle to overcome or a tough goal to achieve? Maybe when his team is behind in a game, your child suddenly evolves into a dynamo leading the others to the win. Or perhaps, if she were cut from a team or made a disappointing grade in school, you saw her determining to work even harder to improve for next year.

I think of Michael Jordan here, who was cut from his high-school basketball team on his first tryout. Also, on several occasions when he had the flu before a game, it usually meant he'd score more than fifty points!

Motivated by Creativity?

When you tell your child to do something, do you find that her method of accomplishing the task is often different from the way you would have done it? Creativity is more than the urge to color outside the lines. It's the drive to express something in a new way. Sports can be an outlet for that desire, as seen in a child's unique style of play. But as with all forms of motivation, this one can be applied to any area of endeavor, whether in business, research, art, or any form of craftsmanship.

Most of us are either "push" or "pull" persons. A push is intrinsically motivated and will automatically engage things by herself. So when a dad says,
"My child is just naturally self-motivated," what he's probably saying is, "My
child is a push." The child has a sense of inner direction and significant
internal desire to succeed. Pulls, on the other hand, wait to be drawn into
the action by some *external* factor or person. They're extrinsically motivated.
They may need a shove to get them started, but then their own motor takes
over, and it's off to the races. Whether your child is a push or a pull, you still
need to be involved in the process. Here's how:

1. OBSERVE WHAT COMES NATURALLY.

Pay close attention to what has typically inspired your child in the past. I
was always motivated by personal performance goals as I was growing up.
Others are motivated by overcoming obstacles or by taking on bigger challenges, but that wasn't me. I just wanted to do well and know that I was
constantly improving. As I discovered more ways to gauge my effectiveness, winning became less a compulsion, and I gained more freedom to
accept failure. This way of being motivated certainly reduces the stress of
having to win.

Realize, though, that your children's interests will likely change as they
grow older. This is natural; accept it. We've seen children who will play a
particular sport as little kids and just love it, but when they get to junior
high school, and the level of competition increases, they may drop out saying, "I don't want to play at this level." If that happens, parents shouldn't
say, "Well, you just have to force yourself because we have this goal in mind
for you." Or, "We've spent so much money on you that you can't quit
now!" You see, some kids are naturally competitive; others are more relational, and intense competition is the last thing they're going to enjoy.
Therefore kids need to make their own decisions about continuing to play
at the next level.

2. USE A GOOD QUESTION.

Along with your own learning, you'll want to help your child see, too, what really motivates him or her. Janet uses a simple illustration when speaking to parents: "You're trying to get Johnny interested in soccer, but one day after a game, it dawns on you that he isn't motivated by being on a team. So as you're trying to bring this to the surface for him, you ask:

"Johnny, what did you like about that game?"

And he says, "I like it when I have the ball, and I run down the field, and I kick at the goal. But I don't like it when anybody gets in my way or if I'm supposed to pass the ball to somebody else."

What you both may discover is that Johnny would prefer individual sports to team sports. So you say, "Well, maybe you'd like tennis, golf, swimming, or wrestling better, since those are individual sports." You may have a child who thrives on one-on-one competition, in which case you could explore those options. That's where he's more likely to flourish. So not just with sports, but with everything your child tries, learn to ask: "What did you like about that…event, experience, assignment, project, activity?"

3. HIGHLIGHT THE DEEPER MOTIVATIONS.

Help kids recognize some of the deeper purposes in athletic participation. Are we motivating them intrinsically or using a cheap substitute? Here's what I mean. Hard work and practice lead to winning, just as study and self-discipline in academics lead to good grades. Children need to learn to build on those positive traits rather than focus merely on the end result. In other words, physical fitness is good because it keeps you in shape to perform, not because it means you're going to beat the other guys.

Obviously you've got to find the right fit for your child in terms of how much pushing you do as a parent. Each child has a different level of intrinsic motivation. So you'll want to think this issue through carefully for each of your children. For a little practice, think about how you would respond with each of the children below. Mark each case below with a B, E, or G.

Then plan to discuss these mini-cases with your spouse. What adjustments could you make in your own approaches with your children? Be ready for differences of opinion!

B = The parents need to **back off.**

E = The parents need to **engage the child more.**

G = The parents have found a **good balance.**

___ Case #1: Twelve-year-old Kamisha enjoys listening to music and reading science-fiction novels. Her parents are proud to have such a good girl, who, they say, "has never given us a day of trouble." Most afternoons, Kamisha quietly enters her bedroom and turns on a classical music station. "She loves just about every form of music," says her mom. "And with her at home, I don't have to worry about her getting into trouble, like so many of the other kids at the middle school."

___ Case #2: High-schooler Dan loves to fix things. He's been taking apart—and putting back together!—various mechanical items around the house since he was a little guy. Now he maintains and fixes the cars and most of the appliances in the family household. Bill and Sue, his parents, have set up a workshop for him in the backyard. They've also told their friends they can bring their cars over for repairs. Often, when Dan gets home from school, one or more cars are waiting for his attention.

___ Case #3: Seven-year-old Johnny always enjoyed tussling with his little brother on the living room floor. So his Dad decided to take him over to the junior high where they were starting a PeeWee wrestling club. After the first practice, Johnny said: "Dad, my neck hurts, and I kinda twisted my ankle. Do I gotta go back next time?"

PARENTING POINT

HOW TO MOTIVATE YOUR CHILD:

1. Observe what lights your child's fire.
2. Find out what he or she likes about certain aspects of a sport or other activity.
3. Respond, with support, to the signs of inspiration and motivation that you see.
4. Encourage him or her in the direction of particular sports—or other activities—that offer these things.
5. Watch for anxiety or frustration. You may need to suggest a change of direction or explore new activities.

STRIVING FOR PERFECTION...OR JUST EXCELLENCE?

Dr. Kevin Leman, a popular psychologist and parenting writer, has made the point that being a perfectionist and desiring excellence are not the same. It's a subtle distinction that we parents can miss. But distinguishing the two can make a big difference in how we treat our kids.

We need to understand this because some of us have children with perfectionistic tendencies that seem to dog them and make them miserable. They just can't relax and be satisfied with any result less than perfection. In those cases it's not a matter of finding a way to motivate; it's the challenge of discovering ways to help our performance-plagued, perfectionistic child learn to relax and enjoy life a little more. Here we are, back to the importance of fun! These kids need to realize that perfection is unattainable; striving for excellence is the better goal.

Exactly how do you respond to a perfectionistic child when she feels depressed at her supposedly poor performance? First, realize that just saying the right thing won't do much good. Instead, over a period of time, try to demonstrate by your willingness to listen and empathize, that you truly value your child for *who* she is over *what* she does. You see, perfectionism is essentially an esteem problem. We build esteem, not by telling a child how

PERFECTION OR EXCELLENCE?

Here's a chart, adapted from one of Kevin Leman's books, that can help you keep the perfection/excellence distinction in mind as you work with your highly motivated child.[1]

Perfectionists	Pursuers of Excellence
• Reach for impossible goals	• Enjoy meeting high standards within reach
• Value themselves by what they do	• Value themselves by who they are
• Get depressed and give up	• May experience disappointment but keep trying
• Are devastated by failure	• Learn from failure
• Remember mistakes and obsess about them	• Correct mistakes and learn from them
• Can only live with being number one	• Are happy being number two if they know they tried their hardest
• Hate criticism	• Welcome criticism
• Have to win to keep high self-esteem	• Can finish second and still have a good self-image

good she does—which the perfectionist will argue with any way!—but by helping her feel our unconditional love.

You can't argue with "I played *terrible!*" No amount of logical reasoning or focusing on the good plays will change this child's mind. That's not your purpose anyway. What you want to do is work with her feelings. So listen, listen, listen. Then reflect back the feelings you sense. Use statements like:

- You're feeling frustrated right now about how you played, huh?
- Boy, it must hurt when that happens.

- So you really wish you'd have moved to your right? That's tough, isn't it?
- You're sad about the loss, is that it?
- What disappointment! That feels bad, I guess.
- That's a downer, all right. I can tell you're really feeling it.

With perfectionists, give plenty of eye contact, provide your full attention, and use soothing touch. But don't argue about performance. This child may have scored twenty points but will focus only on the one pass she threw out of bounds. In this case, a warm hug will go over much better than an inspiring pep talk from Mom or Dad.

LETTING THE ODDS CALL US TO...FUN!

When I went to play baseball in Milwaukee, somebody had posted a list showing how many people in history have played Major League Baseball. The number at that time was something like 14,583 players. Now that may seem like a large number until you realize that professional baseball has been around for more than 120 years in this country. By the turn of the century, baseball was already our national pastime, and tens of millions of young men have played the sport over the years with the hope of one day going to the big leagues.

Of those, just over 15,000 have made it to the pros, and in any given year today, only about 750 players will actually take the field. What this means is that, of the more than five million kids who participate in organized baseball in this country each year, a mere handful will ever play in the pros. If you calculate that out, the odds would be about 0.00015 to 1, which is an impossibly small number, statistically speaking.

The odds are much the same in basketball, hockey, football, and other team sports and probably much higher in individual sports such as golf, tennis, and track and field. That doesn't mean no one ever makes it. Some will. But before you start putting a lot of pressure on your kids to achieve success in their sport, you should know that there might be a limit to how far he or she can go. That's not pessimism; it's simply being realistic.

So parents, please reconsider the attitude that "you can't have fun and still do well and win." It's just not true. Your whole family will find the sports experience to be much more rewarding if you start today with the single-minded focus of just having fun.

DEVELOPING THE FAMILY GAME PLAN

STEP 3: BEGIN ASSESSING THE MOTIVATIONAL MAKEUP OF YOUR CHILD(REN).

According to your observations so far, would you say your child is a "push" or a "pull" personality? Jot down some of the reasons for your answer:

What indications do you have that your child has perfectionistic tendencies?

What practical things could you and your spouse begin doing to help your child pursue excellence in sports and other areas? Record some ideas.

Idea:

Idea:

Idea:

Growing Wiser Through Winning and Losing

Nothing breeds success like winning."

I've heard parents spout that old adage quite often. As if it summed up all there is to know about the value of sports for their children. They say it after a nice win. But what do they say after a tough loss?

What do *you* say? If winning is the only way to succeed or to gain good things from sports, then half of all team members in any given season will be miserable failures. And with this kind of reasoning, I assume that the kids on all those losing teams would be a lot better off in drama club or marching band.

Or maybe we all need a better grasp of the value of sports. I'm sure most of us parents could benefit from a more realistic attitude about what athletic competition can and cannot do for our kids. We can begin by asking ourselves why we want our sons and daughters to participate in the first place.

My answer is simple: personal growth.

Coach Rick Pitino, in an interview on ESPN, once said: "Losing isn't easy, but you have to lose in order to win. You don't like losing, no one does, but the journey is the best part of the trip."[1] That is the voice of wisdom, the voice of a mature approach to life in general. When our children come to see the positive lessons they can learn in both winning and losing, then they've grown immeasurably in a kind of wisdom that will serve them all of their lives. So let's review the issue for ourselves for a moment. What, exactly, are the deeper implications of winning and losing that we can pass along to our kids?

WINNING: ALMOST HEAVEN

There is a spiritual aspect to winning and losing that we can miss in the midst of all the excitement...

During the 1985 World Series, my team, the Kansas City Royals, was down three games to one against the St. Louis Cardinals. Nobody expected us to win. We had already come back from a three-game deficit to beat Toronto in the play-offs, but most people doubted we could do it twice in a row. If we were able to rally and stage a comeback in the World Series, we'd be the first team in history ever to accomplish that feat. It just seemed impossible.

Well, the fifth game of the series got going fast and furious and, lo and behold, we came back and won it and the sixth as well. As we headed for the seventh and final game, an underlying sense of momentum surged within all the guys. I had a strong feeling it would be a runaway game for somebody, but I didn't know whether it would be Kansas City or St. Louis on the winning side.

Bret Saberhagen, our outstanding pitcher and the Cy Young Award winner that year, was on the mound that night. With the first pitch, I could tell how strong he was going to be. He was on his game, and his fastballs were singing. The innings clicked by—six, seven, eight, nine—and suddenly the victory was ours. It was crazy, but it was great!

They told us later that six hundred thousand people filled the streets of Kansas City on the next day for the big parade and championship celebration. I have a picture of our car in the parade, so full of confetti that our kids were almost buried by it. To have come to that place after all those years of hard work was an incredible feeling.

During those last four innings of the seventh game, I think I came to understand what the joy of victory is all about. I was having flashbacks of all the years of hard work, the hard calls, the pain, and all the emotion. When I think of it now, reliving the last pitch and the last out, it still brings tears to my eyes. I saw the fly ball go up, our guy was out there to catch it, and I knew that was going to be it.

But I didn't want it to end. I just wanted it to go on and on and on…

There's no getting around the fact that sports are thrilling, challenging, and demanding all at the same time. They also allow us the chance to experience transcendence. A friend of mine wrote about this in a little devotional magazine he edits:

> The more I watch my high-schooler boys play sports, the more I'm convinced that we're allowed to have our glimpses of perfection here on earth, even before we reach the gates of heaven. Have you ever seen a double play? I mean really *savoured* it? What a delicate ballet accompanies a perfectly fielded grounder to short— over to second for one, then a mid-air pirouette…and over to first for two! I sit back and know that something in harmony with heaven has just lifted my vision.
>
> My friends call me a mystic, but I've come to appreciate such moments of perfection as a prelude to—or a glimpse of—heaven

in this life. This sets up in me the desire to offer thanks, but also reminds me of a kind of ongoing homesickness. Perfect perfection, the kind that lasts forever, hasn't arrived yet.[2]

Can you relate to that? We want to do well. We want the respect of our parents and our peers, and we want to have fun. In winning we experience so many of those good things, and we are called to one response from it all: thankfulness. We can be grateful for the opportunity to compete, for our opponents being worthy and respected, and for the brief moments in which we sense that something more wonderful than this material world must surely exist.

For a moment, we were lifted into the clouds.

LOSING: WE'RE NOT THERE YET!

Losing is tough, no doubt about it. I think of basketball star Chris Webber and how he felt after calling the time-out that may have cost Michigan the 1993 NCAA Championship. At that time he said: "I worked this hard, shooting every day, sacrificed, didn't go on vacations, playing this sport I love. God, why me? Why is this happening to me?"[3]

If winning is a foretaste of heaven, then losing is the reminder that we haven't arrived yet. Even if we win every game, we still sense something missing; the final victory still awaits us.

Most people, if they had really learned to look into their own hearts, would know that they do want, and want acutely, something that cannot be had in this world. There are all sorts of things in the world that offer to give it to you, but they never quite keep their promise. For they are not the thing itself; they are only the scent of a flower we have not found, the echo of a tune we have not heard, news from a country we have never yet visited....

If I find in myself a desire which no experience in this world can satisfy, the most probable explanation is that I was made for another world.

—C. S. LEWIS

We can enjoy our glimpses of the "finish line" while we continue to run the race. And within this broader perspective, we can help our children grow wiser from both winning and losing. Having drawn from the wellsprings of victory and of defeat they will have become more capable and more well-rounded members of the community.

"But Jim," you say. "I'm still not convinced that losing can somehow be 'good' for my child." Well, I agree that winning is a lot more fun; however, I know of at least four good things that can come from losing—

LOSING IS AN EXCELLENT MEANS OF REALITY TESTING.

It pushes us to come to grips with the way things really are. What is it about our team—or about me as a player—that we've assumed was "working"? How can we adjust? What needs to change?

I remember hearing a nine-year-old boy who had just lost in an all-star tournament exclaim, "Losing sucks!" Those words say it all. We like to win, but losing reminds us that we can't always have what we want. It reminds us that wishing for something does not make it happen. That's reality.

I once heard someone say, "I've had a lot of experiences in my life, both good and bad, but I can say with all candor that I have never learned anything of lasting value that hasn't come through adversity, testing, and trial." We don't usually learn important life lessons when we're flushed with success. Maybe that's the real truth behind some of the stories of emotional burnout that I've included in this book. Rarely through the mountaintop experiences do we gain true wisdom and understanding. Most of the time it's in the valleys of disappointment, self-doubt, and fear that we discover how to look deeper, to look up, and to face up to the realities of life. This should help us to let go of the fear of not doing enough or the fear of being a loser.

LOSING WARNS US ABOUT ASKING TOO MUCH.

Asking too much of ourselves and others, that is. Losing forces our children and us to confront limits and weaknesses. The losses help us here:

How much should we reasonably expect from little Lenny? As parents, we are responsible for observing a child's limits and helping him or her to accept them.

At this point they begin experimenting and finding those areas where they most like to work. Coming to know the boundaries and limits of their expertise, then, is actually a form of guidance for life. And you can take pride in seeing your child develop a sense of self-sufficiency, even as she's discovering her own abilities and limits.

Yes, every human being does have limits. As much as you may appreciate your child's talent and competitive spirit, knowing that he has good judgment about what he can and cannot do should give you a good feeling too. You can be confident that he'll know when and how to draw the line between the satisfaction of striving toward future goals and the joy of thoroughly enjoying present blessings. When children are making such sound decisions on their own, we can be proud and thankful.

LOSING CAN GROW OUR SOULS.

Yes, failure and loss can be a means of significant spiritual growth. You already know that, but do your children know it? I've already spoken of this in general above. But specifically, please remember that there's something about suffering that is vitally important for growing the human soul, and it's not a process that's for adults only. In failure we learn to let go of our unhealthy self-sufficiency. We look around for the help of others. We look up for help from heaven. We finally give ourselves a chance to be loved.

> God brings into our lives the *loss* of what we have been holding
> onto, what identifies us, what is "saving" our ego. We are forced
> to let it go and given the opportunity to just be in His love.[5]

The growing ability to accept grace—unconditional love—is the essence of the spiritual life. Kids need to learn it, and sometimes the process begins with organized sports. Especially with losing.

PARENTING POINT

WHAT'S A WIN?
The ability to redefine what a win looks like is often essential to keeping a positive attitude during defeats.

Instill in your Child a Balanced Concept of Winning:
- The end doesn't justify the means.
- The goal is maximum performance.
- My value as a person is never connected to whether I win or lose.

After a Loss:
- Reassure your children of your unconditional love for them.
- Commend them on their hard work.
- Note their dependability.

In the Heat of an Emotional Crisis, Do Not:
- Condemn.
- Analyze.
- Give a solution; instead, listen and respond by reflecting feelings.

Consoling children after a loss provides some great opportunities for conversing with them on an emotional level and responding to them in a positive way when they're feeling frustration and pain. You may say, "I know it's painful when you don't win." And you can also give them your assurance of support when you say, "I'm proud of you. You played hard, and I know you guys were doing your best. We can't ask for more than that." Or maybe, "Don't worry. You did fine, and you'll get another shot at these guys."

Learning how to accept defeat is as much a part of life as learning to be a gracious winner. Ultimately, we learn more positive life skills from losing than from winning. Kyle Rote Jr., one of the best American-born soccer players to ever play the game, put it this way: "What is the ideal of competition? If it's merely to label one side a winner and the other a loser, competition is wrong. Competition is only right when both sides are evaluated on how well they did with what they had." Honestly, what more can you ask? If your kids are doing their best and they lose to a better team, that's nothing to be ashamed of. So help them to focus on what really matters, which is the effort, the integrity of performance, and the learning experience.

HELPING YOUR CHILD THROUGH THE LOSSES

All this theory about losing is great, but I know you're thinking, *How exactly do I help my kid survive those devastating losses?* One of the best ways I know is to start very early training your children in what Dr. Ronald E. Smith, director of the Stress Management Training Program at the University of Washington, calls the "ABCs of emotion."[6] Once these ABCs are mastered, our children (and we ourselves!) can become skilled in changing negative self-statements into positive ones. This helps immeasurably in coping with the losses, no matter how brutal.

Our emotional reactions, says Dr. Smith, don't spring from a situation itself but rather from our *interpretation* of a situation. What we choose to believe about an experience determines whether we feel joy, anger, sadness, fear, regret, guilt, etc. Here's a way to diagram the idea:

A. Activating situation (something happens)

B. Belief or interpretation (a self-statement)

C. Consequence (an emotional reaction to the interpretation)

Obviously, two different people could experience the same event and have quite different feelings about it. Everything depends on how we talk to ourselves about what happened. In addition, we can change our experience of an event by changing what we choose to believe about it. For example:

Event: Kenny sees his coach kicking third base after Kenny strikes out.

Interpretation: *Coach is really mad and thinks I'm a crummy hitter. He'll never put me in again!*

Emotions: Shame, guilt, and sadness.

Remember that the event itself did not cause Kenny's feelings. Kenny discovered this later when the coach walked into the dugout and said to his assistant: "That third base keeps coming loose, and I've been kicking it back in place all day. Think we should call time-out and anchor it better?"

Our task is to dispute our negative interpretations and replace distorted or false beliefs with truthful alternatives. As we eliminate our misconceptions, we can feel the appropriate emotions. Within the whole process, it's best to give ourselves the benefit of the doubt by assuming the best interpretation of an event until we have good reason to believe otherwise.

How does this work in real life? Let's try another example:

Event: Buford is cut from the wrestling team.

Below are some of the alternative ways Buford could experience that event, depending on the self-talk that issues from Buford's interpretation.

POSITIVE SELF-STATEMENTS:

1. I did the best I could, but I guess I still need to work on my moves.

2. There's no harm in trying. And I'm sure to get another chance if I want it.

3. Looks like now I'll have time for a job after school. I wanted to do that, too.
4. I bet Coach would let me be manager this year; I can try out again next year.

NEGATIVE SELF-STATEMENTS:

1. Old man Williamson must hate me; he knows how much I wanted to make the team.
2. I'm no good at this, and I'll never try it again.
3. What a loser I am!
4. Everybody's going to look down on me.

RELATED POSITIVE EMOTIONAL REACTIONS:

1. Increased desire to work harder
2. Feelings of accomplishment in trying; increased hope for the future
3. Excitement about a new avenue of experience to pursue
4. Feelings of motivation and possibility; raised self-esteem

RELATED NEGATIVE EMOTIONAL REACTIONS:

1. Feelings of hatred or desire for revenge
2. Depression and loss of energy
3. Lowered self-esteem; shame and internalized anger
4. Self-consciousness, shyness, shame

If your child is old enough, show this section of the book to him or her and make time to discuss the emotional ABCs together. The key is to start with your children at a young age, demonstrating to them how their thinking affects their feelings. Be on the alert for evidence of negative self-talk, and be ready to gently challenge it: "So you're thinking that kids will look down on you, huh? Well, just as an experiment, let's brainstorm a bit: In what other ways do you think some of the kids might possibly react?"

DEVELOPING THE FAMILY GAME PLAN

STEP 4: DETERMINE TO FOCUS ON CHARACTER DEVELOPMENT, WIN OR LOSE.

Start paying closer attention to your child off the field. Think:

1. What good qualities do I see developing in him or her because of sports participation?

2. What other activities are helping him or her develop character and integrity? If there are none, do we need to look for other experiences to supplement the benefits of youth sports?

3. Is there anything about our child's participation that is having a negative effect? If so, what can we do to remedy the situation?

Learning All Those Life Lessons

"OK, men, listen up. This is it. This is what we've been waiting for all season – the big game. And, as you can see, there is no tomorrow."

Number 33, get in there! We're going with the fake punt—and you're on." Tim sprinted out onto the field, adrenaline pumping. The ball was coming to him, not the punter. He took the shotgun snap and tried to shield the ball from view behind him—one-handed—just the way they'd done it in practice. But then the unthinkable happened: As he attempted to bring the ball back to his side…he just dropped it. No reason. There was no hit; it just slipped out.

He watched helplessly as a speedy defender scooped it up and ran it all the way back, sixty yards for the winning touchdown. Next morning, on the Saturday Preps Sports Show, he made "Blooper of the Week." Over and over again, from every angle, even in slow motion, that ball kept dropping down onto the turf. No reason.

The broadcasters had great fun with it.

As Tim walked into his homeroom class on Monday morning, he wondered, *How am I going to make it through a whole week of "loser" talk?* And the first thing out of old Finkle's mouth, in front of the whole class: "Hey Wilson, what happened?"

Time for focusing on one of those great life lessons that sports can teach, right? After all, we've long heard that one big benefit of sports participation for kids is that it can teach them all kinds of good things about life. But what, exactly, are those important lessons? Is there anything that Tim could, in these moments of despair, cling to for a little relief?

It's clear that sports can help kids learn long-lasting lessons about winning and losing, as we saw in the previous chapter. But there are also plenty of lessons about character, integrity, and fair play as well. And we assume that sports participation helps kids develop habits of dependability, consistency, and follow-through. They find out how to take orders, how to play by the rules, how to stay focused for long periods of time, how to keep on going when they would rather quit, and so much more.

LEARN THESE GOOD THINGS...

Yes, these are all positive skills and traits that will help your children gain confidence and competence for life—things they can turn to time and again—especially when they've just dropped the ball. No, none of these things will immediately erase the pain, frustration, or disappointment of a bungled play. But if the lessons are soaked in over a period of years, they begin to form a certain kind of person, someone who can handle it. That's why, even if our children only grasp half of the things that sports participation can teach, I think it's still worth it for them to be out there on the field. In any event, I'd encourage you, dear parent, to keep your young athletes focused on the life lessons they can learn on the field and court. Have them try these Big Eight on for size.

1. WHAT A CHARACTER

It's true. Sports participation can develop character. When we get our kids involved in any kind of activity, whether sports, music, drama, or anything else, we give them a chance to find out who they are. This is crucial because, after all, character is the ultimate goal. We're hoping our children will become self-directed, compassionate, cooperative citizens of integrity. We initiate them into sports and other activities because we also want them to know themselves fully and to be comfortable with who they are, to have a healthy self-image, to know their strengths and weaknesses. We want them to maximize their potential.

The true responsibility for behavior, however, inevitably rests with the child. In short, we cannot make them into something they are incapable of becoming. And the more we give children freedom to become involved, the more responsible they become. Having the opportunity to prove one's responsibility and accountability is what grows self-esteem as well as character.

2. GO, FIGHT, WIN!

Sports can teach the nature of healthy competition—that giving our best brings great satisfaction, that we can then win with magnanimity and lose with graciousness. Football coach Lou Holtz once said: "If I finish second in the country at Notre Dame, everybody calls me an idiot. If a guy finishes last in medical school, they all call him doctor." It's a humorous statement, but it taps into a serious, unhealthy attitude of fans about sports. Suppose we gave a little more press to the honor of entering the race, to the dignity of competing in the event, no matter the final score? As champion runner Billy Mills put it, "The greatest degree of competition is not for me to compete against you or you against me, but for each of us to reach within the depths of our capabilities and to perform to the greatest of our potential."[1]

3. JUST DO IT

Sports can teach a lifelong self-discipline and work ethic. Sometimes parents see their child putting so much time into sports that they wonder whether that child is just "playing around" instead of learning how to work. One mom of a sophomore athlete put it this way to the football coach: "We hoped Jameel would be able to work during the summer, but you've got mandatory weightroom workouts almost every morning, and then the baseball coaches have a summer league going in the afternoons. So when is he supposed to get a job and learn about hard work?"

The coach replied, "Come down to the weightroom some morning; I think you'll see something that looks a lot like hard work."

A mom like that must take it by faith that athletic participation can teach the things that the other kids might learn on their summer jobs. Of course, you'll want to monitor this! Much depends on the work ethic of the coaches and others involved in the program.

4. I GOT YOU, BABE

Sports involvement surely teaches teamwork, even when a kid competes as an individual or plays infrequently. "I've become a team player by sitting on the bench," said pro quarterback Randall Cunningham. And it's true: Every form of sports participation calls on our children to relate to others in positive and cooperative ways. This is an invaluable skill that applies to every life endeavor.

The most important thing I know about the Spirit of Sport: It instills in us the ability to recognize and appreciate the talents of others as well as the gifts that we have been given and the ability to work with others as a team. It also allows us to face the challenges of competition, learn from our successes and failures, altogether making us true champions in life.

—DOT RICHARDSON, OLYMPIC SOFTBALL CHAMPION[2]

"Well, here we go again. Why is it we can never get through a shift without a fight breaking out?"

5. GUT IT OUT

Playing sports can develop perseverance amidst adversity. All players go through ups and downs in their growing-up years. One thing each child has to learn is stick-to-it-iveness: Either they learn to persevere or they won't make it. They've got to keep coming back after each defeat if they really want to play at a higher level.

Sometimes kids who haven't had it easy in life develop a mental toughness that helps them endure the tough times. Yet the kids who've had it easy, who've always played, or who've never had any problems, may not be able to handle it when the tough times hit.

As parents, we need to realize that we don't have to protect our children from forms of adversity when they are young. It's healthy for them to experience it and to work through it by themselves and with a little encouragement from us. This might help you to grab your seat at a game when things don't always go the way you'd like for your kids. Let them learn their valuable lessons, even in the trenches!

A statement that I've used in some of my talks is, "You just keep show-ing up." There comes a point in time when things aren't going well, or when you're disappointed and discouraged, and things seem to be crumbling around you. What do you do? You just keep showing up. You come to work, you do the job you're asked to do, and maybe nobody sees how much good you're doing; in fact, they may be critical most of the time. Nevertheless, you persevere, you keep showing up, and before long (if you don't let your atti-tude take a complete nosedive) things will usually come around in your favor.

Sports taught me this. And I taught it to my children.

SPORTS TO LIFE

CHECK OUT YOUR OWN FEARS

Every generation has new battles to fight. It's important, then, to look back at our own cowardice and courage and understand where our fears come from. Before you call your child back from the battles of life, ask yourself questions like these:

- Where in life have I been courageous? Have I shared those suc-cesses with my child?
- When did I give up? Have I modeled fear for my child?
- Were there instances in which it was good that I ran away or quit?
- How do I tell my child it's okay to try hard and fail?
- When did I show a lack of courage? If my child knows about it, how have I communicated the cost of this?
- How are my fears different from my child's fears?
- Do I automatically guard against new things?
- What have I accomplished in life that my parents didn't?
- In what areas does my child need to outdo me? Am I holding him back?[3]

6. DON'T CHOKE

Sports participation demands that we face our fears head on—our fears of failure, of mistakes, of embarrassment, and even of physical harm. In sports, the classic way to describe what happens when fear takes control is to say that somebody "choked" or "felt the lump" (in his throat). It happens most often when a player races to the basket for an easy lay-up and then, at the last second thinks, *What if I miss?* Or a golfer tees up and then suffers a fleeting moment of doubt just as he begins his downswing. The basketball clangs off the rim; the golf ball heads for the water. It's the true drama of real life in miniature: Our fears can defeat us. But young athletes can build mental toughness and, with practice and experience, learn to move through their fears.

7. ADJUST OR SELF-DESTRUCT

Handling change and adjustments is a big part of the sports experience. What happens when the high-school quarterback gets to college and suddenly he's not the big star anymore? What happens when the swimmer who took all the medals in college tries out for the Olympics and fails to qualify? That sort of thing happens. It's not a natural concept or an easy one for parents to deal with, because we want to see our kids succeed and be rewarded for their efforts. But we can be thankful for those times when they're put into situations where they have to develop a little flexibility. Those times may be very valuable for them later on.

I've heard professional athletes say things like, "My coach's not playing me during my sophomore year really did it for me. After that, man, I decided I was just going to show him how good I could really be." Orel Hershiser, who was an outstanding young pitcher for the Los Angeles Dodgers and the World Series MVP in 1988, was cut from his baseball team in the tenth grade. That embarrassment changed his life. It motivated him to adjust and refocus—and become a champion player. Hershiser, who had an outstanding season with the New York Mets in 1999, has a real story to tell.

Finally, one of the main lessons youth sports can teach is the habit and lifestyle of physical fitness for life. "My stomach done lopped over my belt," said Mitchell in his Deep-South drawl. That's Dunlop Disease, a problem afflicting too many men and women once they hit their forties. It shouldn't be!

Let your kids know from the beginning that a prime benefit of their sports participation is simply the physical health they can enjoy throughout all their years. It's worth every penny you spend on them, regardless of their scholarship prospects. This is our attitude toward our investment in our daughter Briana's volleyball participation. For example, here's what we've spent on volleyball in this year alone:

Club fees	$3,600
Travel	$2,100+
Equipment	$250
Total:	**$5,950+**

It's been worth it! From the age of twelve through seventeen, Briana's volleyball fees escalated as her skill level increased. Factoring in the sliding-fee scale and further travel expenses, we estimate we'll spend about $20,000 by the time she finishes club play. Is this a prudent investment for possible scholarships? Probably not, but we do it to expose her to high-caliber competition, and she enjoys the recreational and social outlets club play provides. If she continues to stay in shape as an adult, having begun with her enjoyment of youth sports, then we'll be pleased.

RAISE IMPACT PLAYERS FOR LIFE

I hope that in this short chapter I've challenged you to think about how being in sports will lead to the development of your child after she's finished with youth sports. As a parent, your goal is not merely to create a good athlete or to win a few more games, but to help your child become an impact player for life. What do I mean by that? Here are some of the things we know about impact players. Impact players are highly regarded people, because on the playing field…

1. They have steady skills.
2. They perform consistently at a high level.
3. They are a force on their team.

But more importantly, on a personal level, in the game of life…

4. They know who they are as people. Through sports, and through the way they've been prepared both at home and on the practice field, they have a healthy sense of self-respect as well as a language with which to talk about their feelings.

5. They understand "goodness of fit." They know that round pegs work best in round holes, and they don't keep trying to drive square pegs into places where they don't belong. They know themselves. They know when it's their turn to perform, so they're self-managed. And they know how to use their native abilities to their best advantage.

6. They have self-confidence and self-esteem because they know that their motivation bubbles up from within. They trust their ability to perform. When they walk on the field they know—and everybody around them senses—that good things will start to happen.

In light of these things, let me emphasize once again: Your children are uniquely designed by God to accomplish certain goals. If you know that now, then you are already ahead of the game.

DEVELOPING THE FAMILY GAME PLAN

STEP 5: CHECK TO MAKE SURE THAT THE BEST LIFE LESSONS ARE HITTING HOME WITH YOUR KIDS.

What life lessons do you think your child is learning through sports?

Ask your child the question above. Jot down some of your (surprising?) insights here:

What aspects of an impact player do you see developing in your child?

In which of the six impact areas will you plan to help him or her grow during the coming months?

Area:

Area:

Area:

Area:

PART TWO

The Parents

Parents, What Do You Really Want?

"Get up ... one more."

Hector liked almost everything about playing basketball: the running, the shooting, the passing. The only thing he didn't like much was rebounding. Too many bodies bigger than his—with myriad elbows, hands, and fingers—all flying around helter-skelter under those baskets! For an eight-year-old just learning the game, it could be pretty scary.

Hector's fears were confirmed as he emerged from a particularly violent rebounding scrum. He staggered…and then fell down on his back just beyond the free-throw line. He was holding his stomach. Another kid's knee had tried to make a dent in poor Hector's partially digested spaghetti lunch.

He turned green, felt sick, couldn't breathe.

"I can't keep going," he gasped. "Can I go home?"

As Hector headed for the bench, the coach mumbled, "What a wimp! This kid's got to learn to tough it out a little. He wants to go home crying about a little stomachache?"

Just then Hector turned and looked back at the coach with pleading eyes. "Dad," he said. "Can't I *please* just go home and lay down for a while?"

What would cause a dad to be like that with his child? Does he want to hurt the child? Does he want to be mean? Does he want to destroy his son's self-esteem?

Of course not!

But if not, then what does he *really* want? And why is he, like so many parents, putting so much time and energy into organizing, officiating, coaching, operating, funding, and promoting an enterprise that is purely for children? Why do parents go to all this trouble? What are they hoping to get out of it all?

These are good questions to ask ourselves, right? Few of us are as crude as little Hector's dad-coach. That's admittedly a piece of fiction to make a point. But we've had our moments, haven't we? We've certainly had some powerful feelings at games and elsewhere.

To learn to understand those feelings and control them, we must delve a little deeper into our true desires. In chapter 1, I spoke about tensions and pressures that can plague a sports family. In this chapter and the next we'll go deeper into the issue by looking more specifically at the parents—who they are and what they want. In subsequent chapters, we'll ask similar questions about the wants of kids and the wants of the coaches.

But for now, this chapter is all for you, Mom and Dad. In each of the four cases below, see if you discern any aspects of yourself—your needs, wants, desires, goals, dreams. I'll readily validate the "good" wanting. We're filled with all kinds of good and helpful and child-nurturing desires for ourselves and our kids. But I'll also point out how the good and worthy can become distorted and warped. Then, in each case, I'll suggest some solutions—as dos and don'ts—for restoring parental wanting to its proper function.

CASE #1: WHAT A COOL DADDY!

"Hey, Girlfriend, let's go down to the practice range and work on your tee shots."

"No, Dad, some kids are coming over tonight. We're having a little party in honor of Jay's getting his driver's license."

From that moment on, Karla's dad became a paragon of helpful hospitality. He helped with the snack preparation and even rushed to the store to buy paper plates and cups. And when everything was ready, once the other teens arrived, he ended up being the life of the party! Joking, showing genuine interest in all the kids, he kept things lively the whole time.

"Your dad is so cool, Karla!" her guests said as they left for home.

As she closed the front door and headed up to her room, Karla felt she loved her dad more than anybody ever could.

WORTHY WANTING: "I WANT TO BOND WITH MY CHILD."

Good idea: We all want a closeness of love and affection to flow between our children and us. Let's face it, we really want our kids to love us! And that's just fine.

WARPED WANTING: "I WANT TO BE BEST FRIENDS."

Bad idea: Things get a little tricky when our need for love pushes us into playing best friend to our child. The parental role begins to blur. And whether kids know it our not, they are then heading down the road to disappointment. You see, our children are looking to us, pleading for us to give them rules, set boundaries, administer discipline, be the voice of wisdom. Believe it!

Even when a teen's protests escalate into vociferous shouting or copious tears—with door-slamming and wall-pounding thrown in for good effect—kids still want a parent to be thoroughly adult, not just one of the gang. Karla will learn, perhaps far later in life, that her dad failed to *give* her the best by wanting to *be* her best friend. In a sense it was all too easy for Karla, too easy for her own good. A well-known psychologist, Paul Tournier, said it best:

> Parents must not cowardly abdicate their authority. Youths who win their independence too easily, without having had to wrest it from their resisting parents, are very poorly prepared to make use of it in life. In the struggle the child will acquire experience; he will learn how far he may resist and at what point he must submit.[1]

"In other words," says the writer of *The 7 Worst Things Parents Do,* "in a healthy family, somebody is always in charge. When the boundary begins to dissolve, the result is emotional chaos."[2]

WANTING TO CHANGE?

Closeness and love develop between parent and child as a result of the parent's being a mature adult guide and the child's growing in wisdom until it's time to leave home. Notice that I said "result." If we make bonding our goal, we may end up abdicating our authority in the home. What to do? I suggest:

DO work yourself out of a job. That is, move toward eventual separation. Your job is to gradually release your children into self-directed adulthood. Parents who do all the planning, all the directing, and all the evaluating during the growing-up years often feel that they have to solve all the problems when something goes wrong. This puts the child in the position of being uninvolved and less able to deal with the challenges they will encounter later in life. What we're proposing is that the parents should recognize that they are responsible for releasing the child into adulthood. Thus they raise the child to be self-directed, creative, and able to solve his or her own problems.

Kids just can't do that very well when the mom or dad is merely their best friend. Instead, Mom and Dad need to be fully adult role models.

True parenthood is self-destructive. The wise parent is one who effectively does himself out of his job as parent. The silver cord must be broken. It must not be broken too abruptly, but it must be broken. The child must cease to be a child.... The wise parent delivers the child over to society.

—ROBERT HOLMES[3]

DON'T worry if they get ticked off! It's okay. You can't be buddy-buddy all the time. Realize and accept the fact that when you set rules and boundaries, you'll get some anger in return. If not, something's definitely wrong! Just prepare yourself in advance to weather the storm. Later, perhaps years or decades later, your children will thank you.

CASE #2: YOU GO, GIRL!

"Mom! Mom! Did you see that? I kicked the winning goal!"

How do you describe the face of an angel—a little angel who's just conquered the world?

LaTrisha beamed, she sparkled, she radiated joy and excitement. And her mom had, indeed, seen it all. The quick cut to the left, the fake, the little skip, the lightning-flash of speed. And then a boomer kick.

Wow! Mom could only sit back and bask in the glow.

WORTHY WANTING: "I WANT MY CHILD TO HAVE JOY AND HAPPINESS."

Good idea: We parents thoroughly enjoy seeing our children happy. It's a big part of our reward for all the difficult things we do in raising them. (Remember the diapers?) We experience this enjoyment when we see our children having friends, fitting in, receiving nice gifts, making good grades, experiencing anything that makes their eyes twinkle. And yes, scoring the winning goal brings it on too.

If you admit these things…

- I want my child to excel
- I want my child to be happy
- I want to see the joy, fulfillment, satisfaction in her face

…there is nothing wrong with you! These are excellent desires within any parent, and a sign of genuine love for children. I'm convinced my parents wanted all the best for me. They were good people. They cared for me enough to provide a home and a shelter and all the things we needed while growing up. They took my siblings and me to church and cared that we grew up with a sense of values. Those are the things I'll cherish the rest of my life.

WARPED WANTING: "I WANT TO PUT YOU UP ON THE MANTELPIECE—AT THE CENTER OF OUR HOME."

Bad idea: The problem comes when we inadvertently drift into promoting a subtle form of narcissism in a young person. What do I mean? Simply this: We make the child the center of attention, the center of the family, the center of everything. If making our child a best friend is a problem, then making him or her the object of our worship is surely worse.

What a burden for the child! What terror!

I was given more than my fair share of the attention in our family when I was growing up. Sports were so important that at times my needs and interests took precedence over everything else. You might think at first glance that this was a perfect situation for me, since all eyes were on me and my schedule had a priority within the family. But what it led to, in fact, was having to go through some serious reevaluations later on to deal with the kind of self-centeredness and narcissism that occurs for a star player.

I realize now that during my playing years I often hurt my wife and children with my selfishness. Since I've been out of professional sports I've seen that this one area creates some of the biggest problems in the lives of players.

Most of us never dealt with these issues when we were growing up. I suspect this is probably the main reason why so many baseball players are divorced.

Most of the really good athletes in this country have been on a pedestal their whole lives, and they don't really know any other way of relating. The one good thing that happened for me was Janet. When we started dating in high school, she was a cheerleader and I was the star athlete, but she really held my feet to the fire and let me know that I wasn't the most important thing in Galesburg, Illinois.

What a shocking revelation! In some ways, it was refreshing to me, though. I didn't get that message anywhere else. And I did need it.

WANTING TO CHANGE?

If you sense that your child is starting to climb up on the mantelpiece in your family, try these dos and don'ts on for size:

DO take the burden off your young athlete's shoulders. In reality, it can be terrifying for a child to know that the whole weight of the family's worth and self-esteem is riding on her shoulders. Since not only the agenda but also the whole mood of satisfaction or excitement in the family rides on her success on the field, she feels an inordinate sense of responsibility that, in some cases, may lead to depression or self-hatred later on.

DO put your marriage first. Someone once said, "The best thing a dad can do for the children is to love his wife." And vice versa. The centerpiece of the home is the parents. Let that be clear to all.

DON'T think you can save your child from all unhappiness. You can't shield her from every hurt, and you can't heal all of her wounds. Putting children on the mantelpiece won't guarantee their happiness, and it certainly won't save them from pain in life. If they are to find happiness, it will come to them as it comes to all of us: as the result of pursuing other things—their own goals, their own loves. In that process they will surely travel through valleys of hurt and woundedness. But like us, they will no doubt survive. If they are to be happy with life, it must be *their* life.

DON'T give the impression that success in sports—or anything else, in itself —will make them happy. The message I got when I was growing up was that if I was able to make it to the big leagues, baseball would give me fame and fortune and everything that life has to offer. It was that particular message that brought me tumbling down in 1977, after my first four years in the majors. The idea here is that we send a very strong message when we troop the whole family out to see Johnny or Susie participate in sports. If we insist that everybody's going to the game tonight because it's important that we all be there to support this one child, then we're signaling that Johnny is the most important member of the family.

CASE #3: DUELING DADS

"That your boy out there, number 78?"

"Yeah, he's only a freshman."

"He's definitely a big one."

"Well, we bought him a set of weights when he was ten, and he's been working out ever since. He should do pretty well this year. Who's your boy?"

"Number 12 over there. Billy Smith. You know, all-state quarterback last year?"

"Oh."

"What do you do, Bob?"

"Drive a taxi. You?"

"Brain surgeon. See ya."

"Yeah."

WORTHY WANTING: "I WANT TO FEEL SIGNIFICANT."

Good idea: I've touched on this theme already, so I'll just reiterate here that our desire for significance is very strong. We all want to have a sense of well-being and self-confidence. I say, go for it!

WARPED WANTING: "I WANT YOU, CHILD, TO GIVE ME THE STATUS I'M LOOKING FOR."

Bad idea: We want to be able to say, "I am significant because of this or that achievement." But if we fail to achieve that status on our own, we may try to do it through our children. We may do it so we can say, "I'm significant because I'm the parent of a physically gifted child."

For a lot of us, this is a gut-level issue, and we may not like what we discover about ourselves if we dig a little deeper. But we must dig! Because until we come to grips with our own status needs in the parent-child relationship—especially if it involves sports or other organized programs—we are at risk of making some important decisions for the wrong reasons and possibly overlooking some answers that are truly in the best interest of our children.

At heart this is a spiritual problem. For example, look around and see the lust for accumulation in our society today. Why are we such voracious consumers? Can we really build our status by what we own, what we do for a living, or what our child does on the field? No, our significance runs so much deeper than our status symbols. It all has to do with our status with the Creator—knowing we're loved by Him. I like the way writer and teacher Richard Foster framed the issue in his book *Celebration of Discipline:*

> Because we lack a divine Center, our need for security has led us into an insane attachment to things. We must clearly understand that the lust for affluence in contemporary society is psychotic. It is psychotic because it has completely lost touch with reality. We crave things we neither need nor enjoy. We buy things we do not want to impress people we do not like.... Covetousness we call ambition. Hoarding we call prudence. Greed we call industry.[4]

WANTING TO CHANGE?

Is your own status getting in the way of family harmony? Is your ego calling the shots? If so, here are two suggestions:

DO uncover your real goals for your child in sports. We've said that the goal of parenting ought to be to raise a responsible, self-directed, creative young person who will be happy and content, who will be able to solve problems throughout life and to be involved in the community in a positive way. And the parent's ability to come to grips with issues such as personal agendas, emotional self-control, and the child's individuality will make a big difference in whether or not the child will end up enjoying his or her sports experience. The parent's attitude going into it will actually shape and predict the kind of fulfillment and attainment the child can expect to achieve on the other end. So I challenge parents to ask themselves: "What is my purpose?"

If your purpose is to increase your status, beware the danger for your children:

> Let's face it: 99.9% of our children will never live up to our imag-
> ined perfection. If they were to try, 99.9% would most likely fail.
> Those that come close, or continue to try against all odds, often
> pay an expensive price for questing after what they eventually real-
> ize was never their goal in the first place, but their mother's or
> father's. In striving for the success their parents demand, these
> individuals gradually accumulate the symptoms and signs of stress.
> In their twenties and thirties, for example, they develop chronic
> headaches or stomach problems—diarrhea, constipation, sour
> stomach. In their forties and fifties, they graduate to stomach
> ulcers, hypertension, panic attacks, and depression. No matter
> what they attain, they have learned, it will not be enough; they
> will have to strive for more.[5]

DON'T try to control your child's destiny. A lot of parents in sports think that if they can manage and plan and program everything for some kind of end result, then their child will be a star and everything will turn out just great. But that's an illusion. That is not the way it works, and in the process of approaching things from that point of view they may actually do a lot of damage before they finally get the point.

Think of what your kids are actually like. Kids are like Jell-O. You can't pin them down and you can't make them hold still. No matter what you do or say, they're going to wiggle out of your grasp and, in the end, they're going to be what they're going to be. From my own experience, I would say that what they become will often be, very deliberately, something other than what you, the parent, had in mind. At times it seems that kids are designed to frustrate the intentions and plans of their parents.

CASE #4: GOING FOR THE GUSTO?

Truth be told, a guy can do a maintenance job like this mostly on autopilot, thought Fred DiAngelo. He ambled down the stairs and into the boiler room, stopping to check the gauges on several of the huge warehouse heating units. *If the boredom doesn't get me first, I'll retire from this job in a few years—live large on a nice pension.*

But the boredom just might win, after all! He went back to the office and sat down at his desk. *Three more hours until the next rounds —and the phone never rings around here. Must be doing my job a little too well…*

In the meantime, it was time to get back to what he was daydreaming…er…thinking about. *Oh yeah, Darrel's game this Friday night. Now let's see, the Warriors have that big ninth-grader on the offensive line, but I still think our defense can beat this middle school from across town. If only we'd…*

> **CAUTION**
>
> **A DAMAGING EGO-BUILDER**
> One day the child may realize that he or she has been used to pump up a parent's damaged ego. He or she will feel hurt, frustrated, and emotionally abused. When that happens, the parent-child relationship may suffer irreparable damage.

Over the intercom came a soft voice, "Mr. DiAngelo, please report to the second floor."

"Mr. DiAngelo, please report…"

"Mr. DiAngelo…"

On the third repetition of his name, Fred's head lifted.

Hey, was that for me? Probably not, he thought, reaching for his next donut.

WORTHY WANTING: "I JUST WANT A LITTLE EXCITEMENT IN MY LIFE."

Good idea: Who could blame a parent for looking forward to his child's next game with a sense of anticipation? And it's certainly true that into every life a little boredom must fall (or something like that).

WARPED WANTING: "I (APPARENTLY) WANT TO IGNORE MY OWN EMOTIONAL AND SPIRITUAL NEEDS."

Bad idea: When a whole fantasy world (revolving around our kid's next game) pushes out the excitement—and boredom—of our real life, then we have a problem.

Psychologists say that fans often feel the same kinds of adrenaline rush experienced by athletes on the field. And when parents are too connected to their children's on-the-field experience, they lose the ability to appropriately separate. They become unhealthily entangled in their children's lives.

It can get even worse. In a cover story about youth sports in the July 12, 1999, edition of *Time* magazine, reporters said that thousands of parents are physically addicted to the vicarious thrill of athletic performance. The report went on to speculate that moms and dads in the baby boomer generation, some of whom are now in their prime parenting years, are trying to recapture the joy of their own childhood experiences. The problem is that, in this modern age, the sandlot is gone forever and the pick-up games we used to play have been replaced by highly organized leagues with schedules and rule books, box scores and player rankings, professional coaches and referees, as well as designer uniforms with team logos. Everything has become much more sophisticated.

Much, much more exciting!

Relentless fantasizing by bored parents—and the resultant overzealous behavior—violates the basic premise of good sportsmanship and teaches all the wrong lessons. We want sports to be physically healthy, mentally stimulating, and emotionally rewarding for the participants, win or lose, and not merely a means of vicarious excitement for the parents. Unfortunately, the attitude that makes some parents feel they have to orchestrate their child's athletic experience often derives from a need to compensate for things they may have missed in their own lives, especially at work—such as respect, approval, recognition, and the sense of being challenged and engaged in something that is, well, thrilling.

WANTING TO CHANGE?

If you have a feeling that youth sports is pretty much your reason for living, consider:

DO "get a life." Think carefully about this: Are you a whole person in your own right, with your own friends, interests, and hobbies? Or does virtually everything revolve around your child and his or her "exciting" activities? When you find yourself overfocusing on the activities of the child, try to refocus your attitude to your relationship with him or her. You may need to seek career counseling, explore new directions, get counseling to find out how you can be more in tune with your own needs.

DO nurture your spirit. Do you take time to pray? To rest

SPORTS TO LIFE

How to find your inner circle of friends? Ask yourself:

- Who do I feel safe with?
- Who pursues a relationship with me?
- Who has shown consistency with me over time?
- Who loves me unconditionally?

and to be quiet in God's presence? Dale Carnegie said, "We are all dreaming of some magical rose garden over the horizon—instead of enjoying the roses that are blossoming outside our windows today." We all need regular times of quiet and meditation in order to offer thanks and to bring our petitions before the Almighty. We need some quiet space in our days to know ourselves and to contemplate whether our constant busyness has shifted our priorities in unhealthy ways. So guard your time with God!

DO monitor your emotions. We're all familiar with parents who react to every sports event in which their children are playing as if it were the Super Bowl or the World Series. Even in my own life, I've had to ask myself at times: What's going on here?

I had a friend several years ago who proudly declared, "Jim, I never analyze the reasons for anything I do. I just keep moving forward. It's better that way!" But I had to wonder: Better for whom? I had observed this guy's behavior for years. His entire life revolved around an array of compulsive activities. He was a workaholic. His children had suffered one disappointment after another because of his broken promises. They were becoming visibly angry and withdrawn. His wife was remote, sad, and obviously in pain, and yet this man boldly stated that he never analyzed any of his behaviors.

What a huge mistake! No one can grow psychologically, emotionally, or spiritually with that sort of smug complacency. Janet and I have found that understanding ourselves and our impact on each other and our children, gives us a foundation for those reality checks that we all need from time to time. Self-analysis, reflection, and feedback from others keep me honest with myself and everyone else.

DON'T ignore the social side of your life. It's so helpful to have a small group of friends that you can talk to. The idea of small groups and accountability groups has caught a lot of people's interest in the last few years, and I think it's a great idea. People you trust, who you can communicate with and share your feelings, can sometimes say things that will help you get back in stride during trying times. If you have some friends like that, you're a fortunate person.

Let's face it, we human beings were made for each other. One writer put it this way: "I believe God created us incomplete, not as a cruel trick to edge us toward self-pity, but as an opportunity to edge us toward others with similar needs. His whole plan for us involves relationships with [Him and] others…. Loneliness, that painful twinge inside, *makes* us reach out."[6]

DON'T neglect self-care in all areas of life. Most parents, if they are honest, will admit that they want some things for themselves, versus devoting all of their energies to the kids and always saying "yes." But they feel guilty, as if it's wrong to want these things.

Is this selfish? No. Realize that taking care of your self is the best way to take care of your child. When you fly on an airplane and the flight attendant gives her talk about the oxygen masks, the instruction is to put your own mask on first, *then* put one on your child. It's the same with parenting: You must seek to bring a whole, emotionally healthy adult to the relationship so your child can enjoy the greatest benefits of family life. You can do it!

DEVELOPING THE FAMILY GAME PLAN

STEP 6: BE SURE YOU ARE GETTING YOUR
OWN NEEDS MET SO YOU CAN BEST MEET
THE NEEDS OF YOUR CHILD.

On the four scales below, mark where you think you are at the moment. Then think through some actions you could take that would move you a little farther to the left side. As appropriate, make some time to discuss your responses and plans with your spouse and/or your children:

1. WHEN IT COMES TO BONDING WITH MY CHILD, I'M:

BEING THE ADULT						TRYING TO BE BEST FRIENDS

A step I could take to move farther left:

2. WHEN IT COMES TO WANTING MY CHILD'S HAPPINESS, I'M:

KEEPING PARENTS AT THE CENTER OF THE FAMILY						PUTTING HIM/HER ON A PEDESTAL

A step I could take to move farther left:

3. WHEN IT COMES TO FEELING SIGNIFICANT, I'M:

| MAINLY LOOKING TO MYSELF | | | | | | | MAINLY LOOKING TO MY CHILD |

A step I could take to move farther left:

4. WHEN IT COMES TO MY DESIRE FOR EXCITEMENT
AND MEANING IN LIFE, I:

| PAY CLOSE ATTENTION TO MY NEEDS | | | | | | | ATTEMPT TO IGNORE MY NEEDS |

A step I could take to move farther left:

Check Out Your Game-Day Personality

"Spectators in rows A though J, please grab your belongings and proceed to the gate. You've been traded to another ball club."

I n the bleachers on any given day you will see all kinds of characters—quiet ones, loud ones, active ones, and passive ones. You'll see parents who appear to have it all together and others who would rather be somewhere else. They're a strange mixture, but they all make up that indispensable group popularly known as "game-day parents."

You know you're a part of them. What you may not realize, however, is just how visible you are to your on-the-field kids when you're a spectator. Kids see it all. And if you're so visible, then consider this: *What, exactly, are the kids seeing?*

One of the most important skills that sports-family parents can learn is how to see themselves more objectively at the games. Of course, it's not easy to categorize the typical mix of game-day parents, but I thought I should at least take a shot at it, for the humor if nothing else. Maybe you'll see yourself in one or two of the personalities I'm going to describe, or maybe certain aspects of the character traits will ring a bell with you.

In previous chapters, I've been urging you to understand yourself because I believe it will help you respond more lovingly to your children. My plan is to go about this in a playful way here and, if you will, with a little exaggeration for effect. I don't want anyone to feel overanalyzed, but if you've ever sat on the sidelines at a youth sporting event, then the odds are pretty good that you will recognize these types:

Analytical Alice: She's the quiet one. She's just taking it all in. She knows the score.

Broadcast Brad: He's the loud one, giving the instant replays all game long.

Cheerleading Charlotte: You see her. You hear her. She's your booster mom supreme!

Documentary Dan: He doesn't miss a thing. The thrill of victory and the agony of defeat, and he's got it all on tape.

Dutiful Debbie: It's always too early for this one. Yet she follows all the requirements with precision. It's her duty to be here, so here she is.

Passive Paul: Never a response from Paul, either seen or heard. He doesn't miss much, though.

Rambunctious Randy: Here's your basic party animal. Nothing can silence him. First cousin to Broadcast Bob.

Smokin' Sam: He's there. He's watching the game, though from afar. He tends to pace the perimeter or sidelines of the field, often reaching for another cup of coffee or that next cigarette.

These characters—in their interchangeable male and female versions—represent habits, traits, and modes of behavior that Janet and I have seen over the years when our kids were participating in sports. In the rest of this chapter, I'll describe how these various personalities tend to react during the games, and then consider how they could better manage their behavior. In

Person:	Traits:	Possible effects on other parents:	Possible negative effects on their kids:	First impression of them:	Motto:
Analytical Alice/Al	They listen well Counselor-type Discerning and consistent A loyal friend	They'll give their blunt analysis and can be outspoken	Over-analyzing and/or critiquing the performance	"Is there anything you *don't* have an answer for?!"	"Emotional math is the name of my game."
Dutiful Debbie/Dave	Responsible Night owl Always there, even with no makeup or half-asleep Attire obviously not a top priority	At least I have more energy in the morning than that!	Overmothering Appearance could be embarrassing	"Aren't there any mirrors in his/her house?"	"Couldn't we change game times to evenings?"

Person:	Traits:	Possible effects on other parents:	Possible negative effects on their kids:	First impression of them:	Motto:
Smokin' Sam/Samantha	Usually stands the entire game Frequent trips to smoke Shares cigarettes/coffee Personable and observant	Isn't there a non-smoking section around here?	Emotionally withdrawn Smoking	"I wonder when he/she's going to return?"	"This is Marlboro country."
Passive Paul/Pauline	Likeable Caring Even-tempered, but can get explosive if strongly provoked	Does he/she care about being around the rest of us?	Apathy Disengaged	"Are you watching the same exciting game we are?"	"It's just a game. Don't sweat it. Relax and have fun."

Person:	Traits:	Possible effects on other parents:	Possible negative effects on their kids:	First impression of them:	Motto:
Cheerleading Charlotte/Charles	Enthusiastic and entertaining Organized Head of the Booster Club Always getting everyone involved	You *see* them all season long.	Fading into the shadows of their overbearing parent(s)	"Will their voice ever give out?"	"Did you know that I once tried out for the Dallas Cowboy cheerleaders?"
Rambunctious Randy/Rita	High-energy and focused Knowledgeable—sometimes annoyingly so Loud A ticking time bomb	You *hear* them all season long.	Apprehensive around and intimidated by parent	"If he/she says one more word, I'm gonna stick my foot in his mouth!"	"DID YOU SEE THAT?! DID YOU SEE THAT?! COME ON!!!"

Person:	Traits:	Possible effects on other parents:	Possible negative effects on their kids:	First impression of them:	Motto:
Broadcast Brad/Brandy	Full of facts—among other things! A courtside coach Extraordinarily organized Bottom-line, results-oriented	You hear what he *thinks* all game long	Intimidated Worried that the coach can hear their parent's comments	"I wish he wouldn't be so loud when he mentions my daughter's name."	"Move over, Vin Scully!"
Documentary Dan/Danielle	Wants results Behind-the-scenes coach Usually helps with the video highlight film at the end of the season	You occasionally see his/her face.	Stung from their parent's critical coaching Embarrassed by their parent's obsession with their performance	"I wonder if his editing bay has a chalkboard."	"The thrill of victory and the agony of defeat. I love it!"

addition, I'll suggest certain questions you can ask your own children in order to check out any possible problems they may have with your bleacher behavior. If the previous chapters have looked at the general elements of our personalities (in terms of our basic motivations), then it's now time to get specific by heading into the stands for a while. That's where we'll see how parents' personalities come through at game time.

INTRODUCING YOUR FELLOW FANS

The reactions of our eight folks on the sidelines range across a wide spectrum, because their emotional makeups offer great contrast. All parents have their own individual characteristics and responses, and these show up in the way they process their emotions when their child is playing. Whenever they're under stress, and when they become anxious about what's happening to their child on the field, they don't just become someone else; they actually become *more* of who they are in the first place. Pressure intensifies and exaggerates their natural inclinations.

In stressful situations, we tend to operate in the ways that are most natural for us. We revert to the basics. So that's why we see such stereotyped behaviors in certain circumstances. In fact, parents who behave in obnoxious or unflattering ways at a game might be the most surprised to see themselves in action, because they're not really thinking at that point. For example, they may react automatically to what they think is a violation of the rules while others react impulsively and sometimes out of control for no apparent reason.

ANALYTICAL ALICE

As we get up close and personal with this first character, what we notice is an introspective person, the psychologist supreme. She's processing everything and taking it in. Someone might look at her and say, "She's not very excited about this game, is she?" In fact, other characters might actually be a little upset with Alice because she's so quiet. She's under control and doesn't express

her emotions, but if you came up and asked her what she thought about a particular play or about something on the field, you would discover that she has a definite opinion about it. And she's right on target most of the time.

Of all the various characters in our game-day group, Analytical Alice would probably be the one who most resembles my wife, Janet. When Janet is stressed and feels the need to solve some kind of problem, she doesn't start hopping around in the stands. She doesn't jump up and run down to courtside. She's much more analytical than that. Instead of yelling or leaping to her feet, she's more likely to start doing all kinds of emotional math in her head, trying to figure out what's going on and what would be the best way to respond. Her tendency in tense moments is to go into a thinking mode.

BROADCAST BRAD

In some ways Alice is like another character you'll often meet, Broadcast Brad. Alice can give you an instant play-by-play analysis any time you ask her. She's not really missing very much; she just doesn't show her emotions. But with Broadcast Brad, you'll hear everything he's thinking. This guy has no secrets. And while Alice may have a similar view of the game, she won't be giving you a play-by-play. She's not thinking out loud. If Broadcast Brad

is around, you don't even need to watch the game because he'll give you second-by-second details. It can be truly wrenching when it's your child at the center of Brad's critique! You may not enjoy hearing his color commentary on your kid's last play—especially when everybody in the first four rows is drinking it in.

Brad feels quite secure about the things he knows. He has his opinions, and he's proud of them. My observation is that he knows a lot about the game but doesn't always employ the right timing (or tact) in expressing his opinions. Though good-hearted, he sometimes finds it hard to resist engaging his mouth before putting his brain in gear. He can be both lavish with praise and harsh with criticism. He simply says everything he's thinking. (I mean, everything!)

CHEERLEADING CHARLOTTE

Introducing Mrs. Hype. Fun-lover, high-fiver, she's involved in everything, from the booster club to the coffee klatch. She constantly visits her children's

schools. She's a teacher's assistant, a carnival volunteer, and she's the first one with her hand up at the PTA. You know the song, "Put me in, Coach! I'm ready to play today"? That's her motto.

Charlotte is the glue that holds the team together, but there are times when she can drive everyone crazy. She embodies the enthusiasm and spirit of the team, but she can be a little irritating, and you may find yourself wishing she would just sit down and be quiet. The more passive types will go nuts around Charlotte, while those who just need a little push to get them more involved will be energized by her bubbly excitement.

DOCUMENTARY DAN

No one sees Dan's face all season long. He's got the video camera up to his eye, recording everything that happens on the court or on the field. What is not surprising about him is that he really knows the game. Coach supreme. In fact, he's probably not a video or camera fanatic at all. He uses film to study the game with his child, and he's helpful for the team's year-end banquet as he provides all those highlight clips. He's silent during the game but compulsive about filming it. He's got it all: the thrill of victory and the agony of defeat—all on tape, that is.

This guy deals with his energy and emotion by doing something with his hands. While another person might let off steam with his mouth, Dan accomplishes the same thing with a camera. That's his job, to record the game. Sometimes he can even use it to analyze, critique, and improve his child's performance or the coach's decisions.

DUTIFUL DEBBIE

Debbie's always there, but she isn't very thrilled about it. Noon would be early for her to get up. Yet she'll go straight from rolling out of bed to throw-

ing on a T-shirt and jeans. She'll grab a blanket and head out to the field for the game. Debbie's the behind-the-scenes mom who's always around but rarely enthusiastic. Her attitude would be, "Is there any way we could make this game one half instead of two?"

Debbie recognizes the value of supporting her children, so she's there. But she looks as if she would prefer to be somewhere else. She won't be an irritant to anyone at the game. She has a responsibility and won't avoid it, but this isn't her idea of fun. She's likely wondering if there isn't a movie playing somewhere that she could slip off to see. Or maybe she's reading a book while "watching" the game. Or maybe knitting! At any rate, you'll immediately recognize Debbie as the one who's constantly checking her watch.

PASSIVE PAUL

Here's one cool customer. People will look at him and say, "Is this guy with us? How can he just sit there being so calm, watching the same game that I'm seeing?" Some parents who are more active and more vocal may wonder,

"Why is this guy so detached from the emotion of the moment?" The truth is, Paul internalizes everything. You won't see it, but there are times when he's excited about what's happening on the field. But you also won't realize when he's boiling inside. He suppresses those emotions. He's just not comfortable letting it all hang out.

Paul has some of the attributes of the classic passive-aggressive personality. For all his calm exterior, he also has the potential to be more explosive—but you seldom see that on the sidelines. The problem is, he's holding everything in for as long as he can. He doesn't talk at the game, and he socializes very little. He's actually watching. There's a part of Passive Paul that doesn't want anybody to see his cards. But there are times now and then when tension builds up and he lets it fly. I suppose this would probably be the character most like me at a game.

RAMBUNCTIOUS RANDY

I generally keep to myself and don't say a lot. Rambunctious Randy, on the other hand, holds nothing back. This guy is congenitally hyperactive. No matter where you go, you'll know how this guy is feeling. He doesn't need a microphone or a PA system; you'll be able to hear him in the next block. He

can be incredibly positive but surprisingly harsh. He's very loyal to his team, but he acts as if he doesn't know anybody else is around and it seems like he doesn't care. You eventually realize that you're going to have to find a place where you can stand closer to the sidelines or move farther back in the stands where you don't have to look at him or hear his yelling. Sometimes you may have to work at finding that spot!

The difference between Rambunctious Randy

and Broadcast Brad is that Randy isn't much interested in analyzing the action before spouting. He just wants to let you know whose side he's on. But that's the thing I like about Randy—he's so incredibly loyal to his child and his team. He doesn't care in the slightest if he embarrasses the other parents. He's loud and out of control, and you can't miss him. But he's always there to stand by his guys and make sure that nobody pulls a fast one. Need to find Randy at the game? Look over there—he's the one yelling at the ump.

SMOKIN' SAM

Smokin' Sam is not as common as some of the others, but he's around. You just don't see him as much, because Sam processes his emotions by smoking a cigarette while drinking a cup of coffee. He's a little bit of a throwback,

 meaning he's not your typical yuppie dad, but he's there. This is a guy who relieves his stress by lighting up and walking around. In fact, he doesn't sit in the bleachers with the other parents most of the time. He stands down near the end so he can step around the corner and have a smoke whenever he gets tense.

Sam will never drive you nuts at a game like Randy or maybe even Charlotte. Sam just roams the outer perimeter, whether it's inside or outside, picking his place so, at the end of each quarter and at halftime, he can get back and light up. At outdoor events, he hangs out with his buddies, who are usually smokers just like him. He's always running back and forth, which makes you wonder whether he sees much of what's going on. But that's the price of Sam's participation: the more stress, the more nicotine.

So that's the lot. When we look at characters like Alice, Brad, Charlotte, Dan, Debbie, Paul, Randy, and Sam, we're seeing people we recognize.

They're not the only people at a game, but I suspect they are typical of most.

And most of us are somewhere on this personality continuum, with various proportions of the basic characteristics I've described. When you look at the way most people behave, you find that they can't be strictly pigeonholed. They're not just extroverted, or just introverted, but shades of both, depending on the situation. I may be extroverted most of the time, because that's my normal behavior, but I may be introverted at games, because that's how I process my emotions. Obviously, the eight personality types I've listed may fail to reflect the varying degrees of certain traits that we tend to express. But they do show how we tend to handle our nervous energy.

You see, as a parent on the sidelines, you have no real control over what takes place on the field. You're not a participant; you're a spectator. So the energy that revs up while you're watching the game has to be expressed somehow, and that's why some people yell and jump up and down. Other parents do things like analyzing, walking around, giving a running commentary, taking pictures, or smoking cigarettes to use up some of that nervous tension.

HOW DO THEY ACT AT THE GAMES?

Now let's look a little deeper at some of these character types to see how they manage their game-day behaviors. If you look at the quadrant below, you should see two things. First, those on the left side tend to be more passive during the game while those on the right tend to be more active. Second, those on the left tend to be quieter while those on the right are louder. Those on the left side usually don't show destructive behavior during games because they are quiet and reserved. Those on the right are more likely to affect their kids during games because they are loud and highly active.

Quiet	Loud
• Analytical Alice	• Cheerleading Charlotte
• Dutiful Debbie	• Rambunctious Randy

Removed	Highly Active
• Passive Paul	• Broadcast Brad
• Smokin' Sam	• Documentary Dan

Parents' negative influences are not limited, though, to behavior *during* the game but often take place amidst critiques and negative comments *after* the game, whether in the car or at home. Understanding the tendency of our individual game-day personalities gives us a reference point to begin thinking about our possible effects on our children so that we can take some action to be more supportive with them.

For example, as much as Cheerleading Charlotte contributes to the feeling of fun and excitement at the game, she needs to be able to keep things in balance. There are times to cheer and there are times to be quiet and a little more observant. She loves to play and have fun, and she wants to be seen as someone who is fun to be around. She claps and yells, and everybody laughs with her and at her. It's true that Charlotte may have a child who responds to her behavior and plays much better when Charlotte is around. On the other hand, suppose she has a child who is embarrassed by Mom's antics and wishes she would just calm down? During the junior-high years kids are very sensitive to the way others see them, so an aggressive mom or dad, no matter how much fun they may be, can be a nightmare for kids at that time. So parents need to be alert and not simply act on impulse without giving these issues some thought. They need to be sensitive to the feelings of their child, because the problem will arise when the parents' enthusiastic or outspoken words at the wrong times will be upsetting.

You may be wondering, "Why are these people this way?" In general, I suspect, it's because this is how they've learned to cope with their emotions. Some people are more analytical by nature, while others are more intense and volatile. Some bury their feelings while others will let the whole world know everything that's running through their minds. But just because these are often instinctive reactions doesn't mean that we do what comes naturally. We need to be careful about going to extremes in a group, especially during the emotional pressure-cooker times at games. We may have to learn to modify our instincts in order to be more compatible and tolerable to the whole group.

I recall a game a few years ago in which I saw the sort of damage that Broadcast Brad can create if he fails to control his enthusiasm. You know how a sports announcer on TV can get so excited that he's yelling out all kinds of stuff? Well, that's what happened with this guy. Our daughter Briana was playing volleyball, and one of the other parents, with all the classic traits of a Broadcast Brad, was roaming the sidelines. We had come to a point in the game where our kids had made a couple of outstanding plays, and you could see that if things kept up at this pace we were going to win the game.

Well, Brad saw this too, and he was just going wild. He was strutting up and down the sidelines giving other parents high-fives, saying how great our girls were doing and exciting other parents to jump on board. I couldn't believe what I was seeing. One of the things I learned in Major League Baseball was that you never do or say anything that might give the other team a reason to get fired up. You don't want to egg them on or put up a challenge that might become a rallying point for them to come back at you.

Our girls were up by a score of 8-0. They had already defeated this team earlier, and they had gained an emotional edge so that the other players believed they were out of their league. You could see it in the way the opponents were playing. But all of a sudden Broadcast Brad started yelling and boasting so much that he jump-started the other team members and their fans. He made them so angry that they began to play with an intensity and determination we'd never seen before. To make a long story short, they came back and beat our team, 15-8. Our players were never able to score another point. Not only that, even though their players were no better than ours, they went on to beat our girls three games straight.

Enthusiasm is good, no question about that. Pride in your team is good, and any caring parent will have it. When you let your emotions take control and you broadcast them in such a way that it changes the dynamics of the game, then your behavior is not only rude and offensive, it is actually destructive to the whole team. That's one lesson our Broadcast Brad had to learn the hard way.

Dutiful Debbie and Passive Paul won't say things that hurt the whole team, but Paul's own kids may wonder if he really cares about the game. He's holding back so much that the kids don't know whether he's happy or sad. Both Debbie and Paul would be better off finding some way to become a little more involved in the action, as long as they don't risk overreacting.

PARENTING POINT

STRESS BUSTERS!
Want to relieve stress during the game? Try one or more of these techniques:

- Stand up and more around.
- Take a time-out; go to the concession stand.
- Socialize with someone during a tense moment.
- Do mental chores, like personal scorekeeping or videotaping.
- Watch from a distance.
- Distance yourself from irritating people.
- Volunteer at the concession stand, but make sure you can see your child.
- Express your feelings with someone, such as your spouse.

We also need to realize that there's a sense in which parents on the sideline are performing for the other parents. In those situations we're all somewhat aware of what we must look like to other people, and we may act a certain way because either we think that's what's expected of us or because we want to give a certain impression. So what you see on the sideline or in the stands may not actually be the person you think it is. If you met Debbie or Dan or Paul in another environment you might be surprised to find that they're actually different from what you observed at the game. And that only accents the importance of being somewhat open-minded about the people around you. At least give them the benefit of the doubt because, to be honest, you'll want them to extend the same courtesy to you.

So now that you've labeled yourself according to the personalities we've discussed, how will you handle your own emotions at the game? My best overall word of advice is to deal with your emotions directly. Ask yourself, "What am I sensing right now?" First, acknowledge that you're feeling a bit out of control, and then begin pursuing those things that can relieve your anxiety. A lot of times parents will sit there and watch a situation developing, but since they're not free to intervene or get involved, they start boiling inside until they're unable to handle it. What they really need is somebody to talk to, somebody to whom they can express their frustration. Handling boiling emotions at a game—swiftly and directly—will increase the amount of time you enjoy the event. So do it!

Here's where the marriage relationship can help quite a bit. If Dad sees that he's starting to fume and getting angry about a situation, he can say to Mom, "This is really getting to me now, and I can feel this thing building up. I need to get it off my chest or I'm going to explode!" Janet and I have found that blowing up and giving somebody an earful is exactly the wrong thing to do. You don't want to let it go and wind up saying something you'll regret for a long time to come.

Not only will you feel bad about the way you reacted, but an episode like that can end up hurting your child as well. Sometimes I've had to deal with these things the hard way. In fact, I remember once spending an entire afternoon after a basketball game at our church calling people up and asking them to forgive me for what I had said to one person on the court. Losing your cool can be embarrassing, and it's just not worth it.

CHECK IT OUT WITH YOUR CHILD

That reminds me: Briana asked us not to say *anything* at her games.

"Okay, Briana," Janet said. "But I only yell good things!"

"Mom, I don't like hearing you yell at all," Briana responded. "It takes my concentration off the game and makes me nervous."

Briana knows our voices and can pick them out over every other voice in the crowd. But we came to see that from her position on the volleyball court, she couldn't tell whether our yelling was positive or negative. All she could hear was her parents' voices.

Hearing that exchange between Janet and Briana took me back to my early years in the pros. I had hit a home run and was coming around the bases, and there were at least thirty thousand fans in the park that day, all yelling. But I was so sensitive to how I was playing and how the fans were reacting to my performance, that the one voice I picked up on was the one coming from a guy sitting right behind home plate.

He was the one booing me.

I know of other athletes with similar stories. Deion Sanders tells about being in a stadium full of screaming, cheering fans—and the only voice he could hear above the crowd was that of his own father sitting somewhere far up in the stands.

We don't often stop to think about the effect on our children when we're doing "interesting" things in the stands. Like it or not, the kids are naturally tuned in to our voices. Briana will always look over at the sidelines to see her mother's reaction after a big play, and Janet always gives her a passive response—a thumbs-up or a smile—but as a rule she never says much. That's hard to get used to at first, but it's part of our commitment to support our daughter in ways that allow her to do her best.

What are those ways? We've got to ask the kids to find out! So in the rest of this section, I'd like to offer some questions that we can ask our children in order to check out our actions in the stands. (I've framed them as yes-or-no questions to keep them simple. But once you get your child's initial reaction, draw her out with more open-ended inquiries. Just say: "Tell me more about that...")

Keep in mind that as you move through this section that we do not want to limit you to one personality's group of questions. You will want to look outside the group of questions that you think may apply to you, because others—including your children—may view you in a completely different way than you see yourself. Also note that I've paired the personalities according to the broad categories of quiet, removed, loud, and highly active.

QUIET: ANALYTICAL ALICE AND DUTIFUL DEBBIE

Both of these personalities could be seen as quality mothering types. If my natural tendency is to be an Analytical Alice, I could appear to overanalyze or even too closely critique my child's performance, which could push her away from me. I might also come across as not participating enough in the excitement of the game.

If I'm a Dutiful Debbie, then my drive to be a responsible mother for my child might come across as smothering. But I also might be perceived as appearing disinterested.

Check-It-Out Questions for Analytical Alice

- I sit very still at games. Is there another way to show my encouragement?
- I tend to analyze things automatically. Does this make you feel criticized?
- I like to give solutions. Do I ever offer information to you when you don't want it?

Check-It-Out Questions for Dutiful Debbie

- I really like to do things for you. Is my level of involvement too much for you?
- In the morning I just throw some clothes on. Would you like me to dress better?
- I like to be quiet at games. Do you want me to show more excitement?

REMOVED: PASSIVE PAUL AND SMOKIN' SAM

If my tendency is to be a Passive Paul, I could come across as noninvolved or not caring because my appearance seems to be removed from all the excitement. My approach to diffusing tensions gives the impression of being withdrawn. If this is actually the way I respond at home, then I'll have trouble getting close to my children and my wife.

A similar partner to Paul is Smokin' Sam. If I have his tendencies, I will keep myself on the move during games, only talking to my smoking buddies. If I do this at home, I will be like Paul in having trouble growing deeper in significant relationships. The whole family may have to take up smoking so we can get to know one another!

Check-It-Out Questions for Passive Paul

- I may seem a bit removed at games. Does this cause you to doubt my love for you?
- Is there a way I could respond to you that would make you feel encouraged?
- My approach has been for you to take the lead. Would you like me to be more active with you in your sport?

Check-It-Out Questions for Smokin' Sam

- Would you like to spend some individual time with me tomorrow?
- Are there places where you would like me not to smoke?
- Would you like for me to check with you more often to see how you are doing?

LOUD: CHEERLEADING CHARLOTTE AND RAMBUNCTIOUS RANDY

If my natural tendency is to be a Cheerleading Charlotte, I might find, as I previously mentioned, my enthusiasm to be too much for my child. A child who is fairly compliant could feel overwhelmed by her mother and could even emotionally withdraw because of possible embarrassment from something she might do at a game.

Her counterpart, Rambunctious Randy, shares in the same excitement of the game but takes it up a few more notches in volume and adds some "out of control" to the mix. He can be an intimidating force to be around. And like Charlotte, Randy can put some real pressure on his kids. Referees try to find a late-minute replacement when they see him show up; his kids may feel the same way.

Check-It-Out Questions for Cheerleading Charlotte

- I really get excited at games. Does my enthusiasm embarrass you?
- Do you think I'm involved in too many of your activities?
- Would you like for me to take more of a backstage role?

Check-It-Out Questions for Rambunctious Randy

- It's been brought to my attention that I'm loud. Does that make you nervous?
- Does my strong voice embarrass you during the game?
- Would you like me to be quieter at your games? Do I yell too much?

HIGHLY ACTIVE: BROADCAST BRAD AND DOCUMENTARY DAN

We will round out this group of characters with a couple of coaching types. If your tendency is to be a Broadcast Brad, you might be viewed by your child as a courtside coach. Your comments make it all the way across the field. Nothing like having the coach's commands in one ear and your parent's instructions in the other! What's a child to do?

Documentary Dan is similar, but a much quieter version at the game. He, too, likes results, but his children won't see the coaching style until he gets them behind the scenes. Break out the chalkboard, and lets head to the video bay. Lots of work to do. No time to waste! Saddle up your horses; we've got a show to run.

Check-It-Out Questions for Broadcast Brad

- I've been told that I'm intense at games. Do you think I need to relax?
- With all that noise, can you hear me all the way out on the court?
- Are there any adjustments I can make so that you're relaxed during games?

Check-It-Out Questions for Documentary Dan

- I like to tape your games with the camcorder. Do I make too big a deal out of it?
- Do you like to come home and look at the video after the game?
- When we watch the video, do you think I'm too critical of your performance?

HEAD TO THE GAME!

There you have it. Now go to the next game with a little more insight about yourself and your fellow fans. Obviously, there are hundreds of possible variables within these basic personality types, and the attitudes we express may combine two, three, or all of these aspects to some degree. But I hope I've added an aspect of fun to your all-important task of self-analysis. Whatever face we wear on game day, the most vital role we will ever play is that of parent. And when we play our part the right way, nothing could be better for the success of our child.

DEVELOPING THE FAMILY GAME PLAN

STEP 7: DETERMINE YOUR BASIC GAME-DAY
PERSONALITY AND WORK ON TURNING ITS
WEAKNESSES INTO STRENGTHS.

Which game-day personality do I most resemble? How do I know?

What are the strengths and weaknesses of this style? Jot down an example of
how these have come through in your past behavior:

To what extent have I checked out my style with my young athlete(s)? What is my next step in this regard?

What one weakness of my game-day personality would I like to work on? What will I do differently at the very next game?

PART THREE

The Kids

What Do the Kids Want?

When our eldest daughter got married, she presented us with a tribute at the rehearsal dinner that made Janet and me realize what a privilege it's been to raise children. Audra gave us a list of some things she appreciated about us as her parents. Remember, we'd spent hundreds of hours with her at sports events, on road trips, and doing all the things that sports parents do. But only two of the twenty items on her list had anything to do with sports. Here's a portion of that list:

I remember...

Family time at spring training, building sandcastles on beaches, manicures by the pool, pizza at night.

Special moments at the lake house, fishing, cooking beignets, eating watermelons, and watching fireworks on the Fourth of July.

Mom and Dad going out on dates, taking special trips to be together, against my wishes at the time.

Going on road trips with Dad—and his attempts to help me with my curlers!

Mom staying home, juggling everything to homeschool me when Dad was traded to Milwaukee.

Letting me know that I was a priority by taking off time to come and have lunch with me at school.

Mom teaching me how to do my first handspring.

The love and support you gave me when I messed up my guitar recital.

Finding out that Dad had been keeping all the handmade pictures and cards I had made for him safe in a drawer.

When Mom stayed home with me one weekend because of a broken friendship.

Crying on Dad's shoulder after a tough volleyball loss.

The mountain bikes in Colorado, the walks on the beach in Florida, the workouts at the gym.

Does Audra's list surprise you? Keep in mind that Janet and I were not passively involved in sports. After all, Audra had been named the best volleyball player in the Dallas–Fort Worth area during her senior year in high school (though to this day we still don't know very much about volleyball). We were and are a sports family in every way, but our family's sports involvement wasn't the first thing on our daughter's mind.

So what did her list say to us? First, it said that spending time with her helped her grow up with a healthy sense of balance and self-esteem. Yes, she loved to play sports. But her identity wasn't limited to who she was on the volleyball court. Second, it told us how great it would be if parents knew what their children were going to remember fondly about family life years later. Wouldn't that give us a good clue as to what they'd been wanting all along?

THE TOP SEVEN WANTS: LISTEN UP!

You see, good parenting is a two-way street. You can force children to do your will, but you can't force them to respect you after they leave home. You must earn their respect over the years by showing that you genuinely care for them and that you're actively interested in what they care about. Given all that, it's only fair that our kids should be able to tell us what they would like us to know as they're growing up. So what follows is our Top Seven list of things that young people in sports programs have told us they'd like you, their parents, to know:

1. WE WANT YOU TO REMEMBER: COACH IS OUR BOSS HERE.

The coach really is in charge at game time. And our kids want us to know that they are together on things with the coach and the team. They want to focus on the coach at game time. Kids wish their parents would respect this relationship. They don't need their parents involved in the player-coach relationship or to be their advocate on the field.

Sometimes parents try to create a pecking order and attempt to influence which kids get more or less playing time; however, the coaches and the team really have a better grasp of who can make the best contribution under the circumstances. In light of this, the challenge for us parents is not to get in the way.

I want to pause for a little damage control with some of you parents regarding the previous paragraph. Realize that there is such a thing as a "genetic rarity." I'm referring to those naturally gifted and extraordinary athletes who come around only once in a great while. Let me name a few: Tiger Woods, Michael Jordan, Dot Richardson, Nolan Ryan, Florence Griffith Joyner, John Elway, Wayne Gretzky, Tara Lipinski. Should I go on? This is a warning to parents who try to put their child up against the performance of a genetically gifted athlete. If you do this, you and your child are in for a miserable time in sports.

Now I admit that, from the outside, it would seem that these champions have become successful simply because they were pushed and prodded by their parents. While my personal belief is that they still would have been champions without their parents' overzealous involvement, I also admit that it's possible they might not have achieved the same level of success on their own.

But, in any event, is it worth it if the child turns out to be a basket case?

Without all the pushing and prodding, the stars might actually have been happier and less confused. If they'd been performing out of sheer love of the game, maybe they could have coped better with the stresses they were destined to encounter. So parents, don't get in the way. Especially, don't get between your child and her coach. Nobody wants that, not even your child.

2. WE WANT YOU TO REALIZE THAT YELLING DOESN'T HELP.

Kids wish parents wouldn't yell at them when they're competing. Sounds reasonable and rather obvious, right? Yet why is it so hard for many of us to hold back?

I'm amazed at the number of parents who bark orders and yell negative comments to their children from the sidelines. We see them pacing up and down the court at volleyball games. They get angry and shout at coaches, players, and the opposing team—and they actually think they're having a positive effect! Some moms and dads apparently think this is what sports is all about. And if their team wins, that only encourages more bad behavior. An apparent correlation between bad behavior and winning reinforces all the wrong messages.

Who of us could be yelled at like that at work, or be verbally abused as we're doing our jobs, and still perform at optimum levels? And what does that sort of behavior model for our children? At times like that, the kids "hear" a lot more from our actions than from our words. The Bible counsels fathers, "Do not exasperate your children" (Ephesians 6:4). These words certainly apply to youth sports, where self-esteem is such a big part of the equation. The other side—the opposite side, in fact—is to use every opportunity to bless our children.

Janet tells me there is absolutely no research in psychology to support the idea that being angry and

critical has a positive motivational effect on a player's performance. Positive feedback on skills and game strategies, even if it's offered in the context of a poor performance, is beneficial. But criticizing and raging are self-defeating and do nothing to improve players' skills and behaviors. So next time you're tempted to emulate some well-known coach by throwing a fit (in an attempt to motivate), think again! My suggestion is that you affirm and reward your kids after the game, and if you have an important suggestion to help them improve their play, then recognize that they'll be much more receptive a day or two later. Wait until the emotion of the game has passed.

The point is, parents need to abide by a few basic rules as they sit in the stands. I came across a newspaper article that made just this point. It seems that in West Palm Beach a youth athletic association had so much trouble with parental boorishness that it developed a parent's code of conduct. The league also provides an hourlong ethics class, mandatory for at least one parent per family, to be taken before each season begins. The classes teach parents how to behave on the sidelines.

Do you know anyone who could benefit from such a class?

Nicole Balogh, 14, who plays softball, basketball and soccer, says the classes are a good idea. "A lot of parents open their mouths and give too much of their opinion," she said. "In some cases, they hurt players' feelings."

"The kids are getting embarrassed every day by the parents," said Jeff Leslie, volunteer president of the association. "We've had instances of little kids in softball crying on the mound because the parents embarrass the stew out of them."

Although there haven't been any major incidents in [this] area, about 20 miles north of West Palm Beach, there have been small skirmishes with big potential. "We have had parents that have been ejected from games. We've had coaches ejected from games," Leslie said. "To my knowledge we've never had a parent physical confrontation, but we've had parent shouting matches."

That was not the case earlier this week in nearby Port St. Lucie, when a soccer coach was charged with simple battery for head-butting a referee, police said. And in the wealthy Fort Lauderdale suburb of Weston, two coaches and seven players have been expelled from a youth football league after police broke up a melee Nov. 6.[1]

My suggestion is that we take the kids' desires to heart and abide by a few basic nevers and always of parental ethics at game time. Here are some examples (I've left blank spaces so you can add your own experiences, based on your observations at games):

- Never yell instructions, advice, or coaching tips to your child during the game.
- Never denigrate another player on your team or on the opposing team—even in conversation in the stands.
- Never question a coach's strategies, decisions, or overall skills in public; if you have a beef with the coach, make an appointment to see him or her in private.
- Never use sarcasm in a "cheer."
- Never verbally abuse an umpire or referee.
- Never use whining, disparaging questions in your conversations

with other parents (for example: Why can't he just make a play? Why don't we ever bunt? Why doesn't she put in number 33? Why do we always use up our time-outs?).

- Never _____.
- Never _____.

- Always be willing to cheer for a good play, no matter which team makes it.
- Always help others appreciate the skill and effort of all the athletes involved in the competition.
- Always accept a win with humility.
- Always accept a defeat with good-natured sportsmanship.
- Always be ready to give credit to adult volunteers; they give so much of their time and energy.
- Always remain quiet when in doubt as to the helpfulness of a contemplated comment or cheer.
- Always show interest in other parents and their children as persons and as families. We do have lives outside the game, remember?
- Always _____.
- Always _____.

3. WE WANT YOU TO KNOW WHO WE REALLY ARE.

Kids want us to know them as individuals with unique interests and talents. Audra's interest in volleyball had almost nothing to do with us as parents. But it had everything to do with her own design and the way God had created her. If you have more than one child, then you will know how unique each of your offspring can be. It's really astonishing. Whenever we'd go into Audra's room, it would be organized. We never had to tell her to study for tests or to do her homework. We never had to tell her to put her stuff away or clean her room. She was just naturally organized and diligent. That's her design.

Our son, Aaron, on the other hand, had a different approach to house-keeping—using the "pile method." And he had to be encouraged to get motivated and involved in other activities. He needed to be pulled into things, but once we got him involved in a particular sport or activity then he would enjoy himself and have a lot of fun. Aaron was interested in being outside as a child. We encouraged his participation in soccer, football, basketball, and baseball. He loved all kinds of activities and needed very little organization. He was a curious child, always creating bike paths in the woods or working with his hands or just taking things apart. The point is, we learned that our role with Aaron should be very different than with Audra.

A passage in the Bible says, "Teach your children to choose the right path, and when they are older, they will remain upon it" (Proverbs 22:6, NLT). Some people think this verse only refers to spiritual values and moral choices, but Janet and I apply it to a much broader range of issues. We hear it saying, "Find out who your children are and how God made them, then help them to choose the right path. Encourage them to develop their skills and perspectives as they grow up, and not only will they not 'depart' from it, they will honor you for what you've done. And they'll want to be around you even after they've begun their own families."

Along similar lines, remember that we each have an inborn need to find purpose and meaning according to our design. So encourage your children to work within their areas of giftedness. Not long ago I heard a well-known Olympic sprinter give a motivational talk to a group of girls. She said, "You can be anything you want to be." How many times have you heard that message? More than once, I suspect. While I appreciate the spirit of her words, I really believe we do our children a disservice when we say things like that, because it simply isn't true. Certainly, a 6-foot-5-inch, 200-pound high-school lineman will never be a great jockey—no matter how badly he'd like to race a horse in the Preakness some day!

I can use my own case as an example. I always wanted to be a home-run hitter but I never made it. It wasn't because I didn't want it bad enough; I spent nearly five years of my career trying to be one. It wasn't that I didn't have the opportunity; I played in more than eight hundred Major League games during those years, and I spent countless hours in the batting cage working on my swing. But I discovered that I wasn't gifted at hitting home runs. No amount of effort could change that fact.

We set our kids up for confusion and disappointment when we say the only thing standing between them and their dreams is having a desire to be the best in something they're not gifted to be. I know the young Olympian meant well in her statements, and in light of all that she had achieved in sports, it was inspiring to hear her say it. But the better things for our children to hear come from parents and other respected adults who really know them as individuals. Then, as appropriate, we encourage them to pursue their dreams within the particular strengths that have become obvious.

One of the things you can do with the sports experience is to use games and recreation as a way of uncovering your child's unique calling. If nothing else, his disinterest or lack of skill in sports may help you to know he's not going to be a baseball player! That, in itself, can be a positive thing.

"As my old skleenball coach used to say: find out what you don't do well—and then don't do it."

—ALF, ALIEN TV CHARACTER

4. WE WANT OUR TRAINING TO HAVE LIMITS.

The kids say, "Mom and Dad, there's a limit to how much training we can take!" Often parents will push kids into one camp or training session after another when the youngsters are physically (and mentally?) exhausted. Teenagers especially have a great need for sleep as their bodies perform amazing growth spurts. Sometimes their homework, sports, and work schedules conspire to deprive them of much-needed sack time. They want Mom and Dad to respect their judgments about when they need training and when they just need a nap! They're saying, "Trust me to know my own body."

It would be good for us parents to stop and remember the rights of our children when we get so caught up in our roles as "managing directors" of their lives. In this regard, I came across a statement put out by the National Association for Sport and Physical Education that all of us can take to heart. Pay particular attention to Right Number 10.

Bill of Rights for Young Athletes

1. The right to participate in sports.
2. The right to participate at a level commensurate with each child's developmental level.
3. The right to have qualified adult leadership.
4. The right to participate in safe and healthy environments.
5. The right of children to share in the leadership and decision-making of their sport participation.
6. The right to play as a child and not as an adult.
7. The right to proper preparation for participation in sports.
8. The right to an equal opportunity to strive for success.
9. The right to be treated with dignity.
10. The right to have fun in sports.[2]

5. WE WANT YOU TO AVOID OVERPROTECTING.

The flip side of the coin brings balance to the parent-child relationship. Some of us are simply overprotective. We stifle potential by fearing for our child's safety, both physically and emotionally. As our kids grow older, we must learn to let them take the risks naturally accompanying any attempt at a worthy goal.

How can we know if we've fallen into the overprotection trap? For one thing, we can ask ourselves questions like these:

- When I look at the situation with total objectivity, how risky is it?
- What would be the benefits to my child in spite of the risks? From her perspective, might this risk be worth it?
- How much of this decision can I legitimately leave to my child?

Have I taken too much on myself here?

- Is my sense of my child's fragility a bit overblown? Is she stronger than I think? Who else can I ask about this?
- To what extent am I merely responding to the fears and/or shame of my own childhood (or adulthood)?

Another thing we can do is be on the lookout for the subtle signs of overprotection. This chart, adapted from the excellent book *Receiving Love*, by Joseph Biuso and Brian Newman, should help.[3]

ARE YOU OVERPROTECTING YOUR CHILD?		
The overprotected child:	**Some signs that you are overprotective:**	**Ways to start letting go:**
Usually refuses to play with peers; would rather be with a parent.	You are virtually the only parent who still escorts your child to school or waits for the bus.	Notice responsibilities and skills your child's peers have been given. Could your child do these things as well?
Looks to the parent(s) to solve problems with siblings, friends, teachers.	You find fault with your child's friends and parents.	Pay attention to the risks your child's peers are permitted. Are your prohibitions making your child feel delicate, accident-prone, or like a baby?
Depends on parent(s) to pick out clothes and get dressed.	You are quick to justify doing things for your child that other children are doing for themselves.	Listen closely to what your child asks to do. Consider what motive for personal or social maturity may be behind it.
Could be characterized as clingy.		Remember that school is your child's territory. Don't expect to be told everything.
		Help your children find solutions to their own problems. And don't make a non-issue into a big deal.
		Maintain time and places for your child to be alone. Everyone needs privacy.

Kids want to direct their own energy, and they wish parents knew that they will ask for help when they need it. According to our random survey conducted in suburban Dallas–Fort Worth, when kids are completely honest about what they're wanting out of the sports experience, they tell parents the following:

What kids say are the MOST enjoyable aspects of playing sports:

Boys

1. Relationships
2. Having fun
3. Competition
4. Developing character

Girls

1. Relationships
2. Developing character
3. Competition
4. Having fun

What kids say are the LEAST enjoyable aspects of playing sports:

Boys

1. Losing
2. Pressure from parents
3. Degrading comments about performance

Girls

1. Losing
2. Time commitment
3. Pressure from parents

'Nuff said?

7. WE WANT YOU TO BE THERE SO WE CAN TOUCH BASE.

A little girl, still a toddler, was running around the house tagging after the older children, just playing quietly. But every few minutes she would come running back into the room where all the adults were sitting. She would go over to her daddy and grab his leg, look around for a second or two, then wander off again to find her playmates. She'd be gone for ten minutes or so and then come running back, grab Daddy's legs, and go through the same routine.

After three or four of these little excursions, one of the other adults asked, "What's going on there?"

The little girl's mother responded, "Oh, she's just touching base."

Another woman said, "What does that mean?" and the young mother explained, "She just wants to know that Daddy's still here and that everything's okay. Then she'll go off and play. As long as she can come back and touch base, she feels safe."

Remember, your kids are human beings, not human doings. What your children need most is reassurance that you're there. If they're doing well, they want you to be there. If they're in competition and losing badly, then they want to know that you're there. So long as you're there to support and not to criticize, they have confidence to go out and play the game and eventually enter the adult world.

THE BOTTOM LINE: JUST LOVE US!

Too often we send the message that we love our children only when they perform well on the field, which is a terrible thing to do. But when kids are pressured to meet unrealistic standards, they may respond by presenting a false self. If the child has to perform in a certain way to get your love, then he may take on traits and behaviors that are alien to his nature, just to gain your approval. Surely we should see that this will produce nothing but frustration and anxiety, and ultimately it will lead to failure and bad feelings.

I suspect this is the main reason children bond so quickly with grandparents. Grandparents have nothing to prove. They're not putting demands on the child. In many cases, they're secure because they've already done their thing; they've raised their kids, and they've learned to be content with who they are as people. And they love the child with an unconditional love because of who she is, as a person and a child of God.

Moms and dads, we can do it! Steven Spielberg's mother, Leah Adler, understood what it meant to make her now-famous son feel loved and important. "I listened to what he said, took whatever he wanted to do seriously, and always made him feel important." Like the time the adolescent filmmaker was directing a big scene and wanted to create an explosion in Mom's kitchen. "He prompted me on cue to hurl cans of cherries in the air. The juice never came out of the wood. But it never occurred to me not to do it."[4]

How do you convey unconditional love to your child? Psychologist Ross Campbell stresses that children must *feel* our love, not just *know* it. He says we can do it in four specific ways, which I'll try to summarize in the next few paragraphs.[5]

WARM EYE CONTACT

Looking into our children's eyes conveys love like nothing else. It actually fills their emotional tanks and nourishes their souls. So when they talk, we give them eye contact. When we talk, we look directly at them. Do we love them? They can feel it in our eyes!

Your child will look into your eyes for subtle messages, and in sports he or she will want to know if there's a difference in your attitudes and affections between the victory last week and the loss this week. When she looks over to the sidelines, is she seeing a parent who is raging, ranting, and scolding or covering her face with her hands? Or is she seeing a look that says, "I know! That was a tough break. I'm sorry too. But don't worry. You're doing great, and I'm proud of you." That's the look she's hoping for.

If you want your children to shut down and shut you out of their hopes and dreams, then make sure they know how offended you are every time there's a bad play or an error on the field. Simply withhold eye contact; nothing will put up a wall between the two of you faster than that.

APPROPRIATE PHYSICAL TOUCH

From their earliest days, children need physical contact. Numerous studies have proven this to be true—even showing that when infants are deprived of physical touch they're in danger of just wasting away! But, parents, remember: *No child ever grows out of this need.* True, the type of physical contact will change as kids grow older. This is true especially for boys, who will gladly receive hugs and kisses up to about age eight, but then they will graduate to playful wrestling, backslapping, tussling, etc.

Here's a practical suggestion: Why not get into the habit of giving your young athlete leg massages regularly? Laying your hands on them in appropriate ways conveys your love without a word needing to be spoken. Your hands say it all.

Listen to how one parenting writer experienced this when he was a child:

> I can still see those pretty grey eyes smiling back at me. They belonged to Miss Hempstead, the best high school English teacher a kid could have. Why such accolades? For one thing, I knew that when I walked up to talk to Miss Hempstead there'd be nothing more important to her than *this precious moment* when I had something to say…. You see, as we conversed, the whole world revolved around me—yes, *me!*—though time came to a complete standstill. For as long as I wanted to be King of the Earth.[6]

When we turn our attention to our kids, let's make sure that our full attention is on them—for as long as needed. This was an issue in my family, a problem that flowed from being stretched and overstressed by my career. The problem wasn't so much being away on road trips; rather, it was that so often, even when I was home, I still wasn't there for them. I'd get these faraway looks because I couldn't focus on what was going on around me. I was totally isolated in the game of baseball.

At the rehearsal dinner for our son's wedding, Aaron offered some very loving remarks about his mom and me. At one point he said, "Dad, I know you weren't there at times." I was on road trips, back and forth practically all year, every year when he was growing up. But as he was speaking those words I was thinking, *Yeah, not only was I not there at those times, but when I was there I wasn't there.* Quite the opposite of focused attention!

STRUCTURE AND DISCIPLINE

Kids long to have limits on their behavior, boundaries on their adventures, and consequences for their wrong actions. As much as they may protest, it's true. The teen, for instance, who knows he's unloved, is the one who can do anything he wants at any time with any person. He knows only too well:

Mom and Dad just don't care enough to give me rules. In contrast, we convey love when we pursue answers to questions such as, "Where are you going? Who will you be with? When shall we expect you back?"

Folks, love them enough to set the rules. Love them enough to hold them accountable.

DEVELOPING THE FAMILY GAME PLAN

Set up a time to ask your child(ren) about the things they want from you, from the family, and from sports. Record their responses here:

Discuss with your spouse which of the seven "wants" of children seem to apply most directly to your own child(ren)? How?

Choose two or three of the kid-wants above that you'd like to supply to a greater degree in the days ahead. What will you plan to do?

First:

Second:

Third:

Let's Talk

"This game is so violent. ... I'm frightened. Hold me."

I went to play baseball at the University of Iowa in 1970. It was the first time freshmen could play varsity ball. Not only did I make the team, I started and was selected as second-team All Big Ten. After the season, I came back home to Illinois to play in the summer league in my hometown. As I mentioned before, the field was right across the street from where I grew up. I felt good about it, but I got off to a lousy start. I was hitting under .200, and the coach benched me.

Well, that did it. I remember seeing my dad and the coach standing down by the left field line arguing right in the middle of a game. And I remember sitting there in the dugout, feeling horrible about it. My emotions were all tangled up.

I made sure they stayed bottled up, too.

As I've described earlier, whenever I felt tired or anxious about something, I would just turn off whatever was uncomfortable for me. Part of the fallout of that kind of reaction to pressure was that it affected my relationship with Janet and our children for years to come. I always reacted with a sort of survival instinct, turning off my emotions and isolating myself from any potential hurt. It helped me cope at a time when I didn't feel I had much control. But later on it hurt me, because I would even turn off the input of love and acceptance that I desperately needed.

Suppose I had learned to communicate a little better with those who loved me?

KEEP COMMUNICATING IN YOUR FAMILY!

I urge you to value openness and honesty in your family, because freedom of expression in the family is critical for the health of your children. The purpose of this chapter is to describe what I mean by that and to provide some practical exercises so you and your family members can be ready to respond when emotions flair up—respond, that is, in ways that will help you all grow closer.

Practicing basic communication principles and skills in the calmer times will help you put them into action—automatically—in the heat of conflict. The first step is simply to recognize the levels of communication available to you in your everyday interactions. Once you're aware of these, you can decide when to push your conversations to the higher altitudes of what I call "top-floor talking."

RECOGNIZING THE LEVELS OF COMMUNICATION

Entering the realm of good communication is like getting onto an elevator. The building has a beautiful luxury apartment at the top, and that is your ultimate destination. But when you walk onto this elevator, you have four buttons to choose from. What level will you usually be visiting, day in and day out, with your spouse and children? What level will you head to when there's a deep need to communicate deeply? These are the options:

Bargain Basement: Here we're usually conversing about the easy stuff, and the talk comes cheap. We need to be here quite a bit, of course. Practical matters are discussed to keep the nuts and bolts of family living from coming loose. In the basement, we find the words that get things done. But becoming too comfortable at this level can be dangerous. Sometimes we need to head upstairs. If we refuse, we'll stay superficial and avoid any topic that might cause the slightest rise in anyone's blood pressure. In other words, we'll stay at a distance from one another by conveniently keeping our talk focused on things outside our relationship.

For example, you might say, "Rotten weather today, huh? I heard they got five inches of snow last night in Riverdale."

And your family member responds, "Oh, really? Maybe the game will be canceled."

Ground Floor: Moving up a level, we exchange ideas and opinions. This is safe talking, with no danger of falling from any height. Yet we've moved higher than simply reporting facts about people or events; we take a small risk in stating what we think.

An exchange at this level might go something like this: "I think we should get the blue jerseys since they go with last year's team jackets."

And your spouse responds, "I'd rather just buy new jackets. Let's try to get a team discount."

Upper Levels: There's even more risky communication here, but it's much more satisfying because we're attempting to know one another better. At the upper levels we dare to share about our feelings and needs. When it's appropriate, we risk saying what feels bad and what feels good. At this level we feel it's safe to risk asking for what we want. We assume that we won't be knocked down the stairs!

The conversation might begin with your son saying, "I feel awfully bad about the coach yelling at me last night."

"That happened to me once, too," you respond. "My face got all red, and I was really embarrassed."

"Yeah, me too. Now I just wish he'd apologize or something. This really hurts!"

Penthouse: Here we've reached the top level of communication, which we can use with those we trust to the fullest. It's the risky kind of conversing that calls for opening up and disclosing who we really are without being defensive. We allow transparency and vulnerability. We can only do this in a context of mutual trust, and we can't linger here all the time. That would be exhausting! But it is our goal to meet here regularly with our spouses, our children, and our closest friends. This is how we grow deeper in our relationships with the ones we care for the most.

Here's how you might begin a conversation on this level: "I don't know if you can tell how ashamed I feel. But I'd like to tell you why, if you've got some time to listen…"

Remember that none of these communication levels is right or wrong. Each has its rightful place in our families. The point is to be wise about when we need to take ourselves up to the next level. For example, if we can't use the optimum form of conversation when it's really needed, we're missing a great opportunity for growing closer in love. Usually it will be up to you, Mom and Dad, to move things to a higher level with your children by inviting more risky sharing through your own example. With your spouse, it takes both partners working at it. Don't just meet halfway; instead, each of you will need to give 100 percent in striving for heightened communication.

WORKING ON YOUR TECHNIQUE

One of the best ways to keep moving toward these higher levels of communication is to practice expressing your feelings with "I" statements. In fact, it's always best to say "I" in a conflict rather than "you," which can easily sound like an accusation:

"I feel hurt by that action." (a report about me)

versus

"You did that again." (an attack on you)

Teach this to your children by example. Try using what I call the that-this-please technique, as in, "When you do *that*, I feel *this*, so *please*… (offer your request)." It's a simple formula to use when you have a grievance and you want to express it without attacking.

That: Say what happened.

This: Say how you feel about it.

Please: Express your desire for the future.

PARENTING POINT

UNCOVERING ORIGINAL SOURCES OF COMMUNICATION PATTERNS

Have you ever thought about the ways in which your own parents' attitudes and behaviors were transmitted and adopted? As you become aware of these early lessons, you are freer to choose the attitudes and patterns that you want to continue in your own families. Take a few minutes and answer the following questions:

- What feelings were okay to express in your family when you were growing up?
- What feelings were taboo? Were some feelings less comfortable than others?
- Recall some of the things that were said to you when you were a child that denied your feelings. How did you feel when you heard these denials?
- What feelings do you have difficulty accepting and expressing now?
- What feelings do you have difficulty allowing your children to express?

Once you discover your basic assumptions and expectations, you have the opportunity to add new information and skills to your parenting repertoire.[1]

Here are some examples:

- "When you slam the door, I feel jumpy. Please close it more quietly next time."
- "When you look at me like that, I wonder whether you're angry. Would you tell me what you're thinking right now?"
- "When the dishes aren't done by the time I get home, I start feeling discouraged about all the work facing me for the rest of the evening. In the future, I'd like you to try to keep up with that chore."
- "When you leave your toothbrush on the sink, I feel irritated. Would you please put it away from now on?"
- "When I hear criticism from you right after the game, I start feeling put down. Couldn't we talk about these things on the morning after?"

The key is to focus on what is happening with you rather than on what the other person has done to cause friction. After all, no one can argue with a report that you freely offer about yourself.

One thing I'm proud of is that we value honesty in the Sundberg family. Each of us openly expresses our thoughts and feelings about what we perceive to be inappropriate behavior, and I've given my family the freedom to let me know when they think I'm over the line. We've gotten some strange looks a few times when Janet or one of the kids would say something to me about not getting a big head.

Fans would sometimes look at them as if saying, "How dare you suggest that this guy isn't as wonderful as we think he is!" But that's okay. Our view was that no one should ever let the praise and adulation they receive as an athlete get out of proportion to who they are as a person.

MIRRORING, LISTENING, AND DECODING

Once we have a good grasp on the levels of communication in our families, we can focus our efforts on paying more attention to one another. With our kids, this requires at least three important skills to learn and use:

First, learn to practice mirroring. Family counselor John Bradshaw wrote a book titled *Healing the Shame That Binds You.* In it he makes the point that mirroring emotions is essential to a child's healthy identity formation. It is, in a sense, the opposite of emotional abandonment. He says:

> Children need mirroring and echoing. These come from their primary caretaker's eyes. Mirroring means that someone is there for them and reflects who they really are at any given moment of time.… Abandonment includes the loss of mirroring and remains important all our lives.[2]

My question is, What kind of mirror are you? Are you giving your child a realistic image of who he is? Or are you reflecting a distorted image? I can imagine two parents who are mirror opposites of each other. One parent only reflects the positive virtues of the child while the other parent only reflects the negative traits and behaviors. It's sort of like the cartoons we've seen of the little angel on one shoulder and the little devil on the other, each whispering subtle messages into a person's ears.

We know from psychology and biology that both heredity and environment play a role in the development of our children. The subject has been debated for generations, but we do know that the environment in which the child spends his or her days will have a profound influence on behavior. Yes, thanks to the role of heredity, there is at least an equal chance that the impact of environment can be reduced and that a change in the kinds of feedback the child receives can help to modify his or her behavior.

Ultimately, the child's inborn strengths and weaknesses will determine the direction of his or her personality. But these inborn traits are often accepted, rewarded, or criticized depending on the personalities and value systems of the parents. What we need to realize is that a parent's reaction to a child will influence the child's self-image, self-esteem, and self-confidence. Therefore, how we manage our children will shape their behavior. How we speak to them will affect how well they adjust to society. In short, parents make the difference in whether or not the children will use their inherent abilities to their best advantage.

We are constantly reflecting back to our children what we see in them, and there's a natural tendency for them to want to meet our expectations and understanding. But if we see them too narrowly, or if we have this narrow concept of what they can or should be, then we may be interfering with the one thing that could catapult them into a fulfilling life.

For some period of his or her life, every child needs to feel that to someone—hopefully the parent—he or she is the most precious thing on this planet. They need the love and admiration of their families. They need to be rewarded and reinforced for good behavior and trained or reprimanded in some way for willful and selfish behaviors. All of this begins with mirroring unconditional affection and acceptance from our eyes.

Second, learn active listening. In her book *Balancing Your Priorities,* Marilyn Moravec offers an illustration that I think says it all about listening to our kids. She talks about the woman who invented the *Ungame.* Have you seen this popular board game? It uses question cards to encourage family members to share about their feelings in a nonthreatening way. Anyway, this Christian mother, Rhea Zakich, had been forced into months of silence by a recurring throat problem. For the first time in her life she had to do more listening than talking! And she invented this marvelous communication game.

It seems she was playing the game with her kids, still unable to use her vocal chords, and she drew a question card that caused her son to offer a strikingly honest answer:

Taking her tablet, Rhea wrote, "Why is it that you share so much in this game? When I used to ask you these things, you would just grunt."

"Well, Mom," her son replied, "in the game we know you won't say anything!"

Rhea says she learned more in twenty minutes sitting around the *Ungame* than she had learned about her family in twelve years.[3]

How do you react to this story? Does it move you to work a little harder at listening to your children? I hope so. But notice I said "work." Active listening requires us to put down what we're doing and fully attend to the child in front of us. A wall poster says, "When I look, let me truly see." We could also say, "When I listen, let me truly hear." And that brings us to our task of decoding.

Third, learn to decode what you hear and see. Simply put, let's try to hear what is behind and beneath the words our kids use. Decoding is paying attention to our children's body language and all their other nonverbal signals to discern what's really on their hearts. Try a little practice with the exercise below, and then go to work with your decoding attempts in everyday life.

Below are five statements that a kid might make. Jot down your guesses about the feelings that are likely to be conveyed. (Note: There are no right or wrong answers. This is just to help you look a little deeper when your child speaks.)

——— ———

Statement: "It's okay if Billy plays second base instead of me," says Todd, as he looks down at his shoes. "I just want to keep the stats today, anyway."

The possible feeling(s) beneath the words:

(Hint: Look for signs of discouragement or fear. Did Todd make errors yesterday? Feeling ashamed? Is Todd being generous and kind, or is something causing him to pull back from a legitimate challenge? Check it out!)

———————

Statement: As tears start to form in her eyes, ninth-grader Krissy says, "Dad thinks I should make varsity next year."

The possible feeling(s) beneath the words:

(Hint: Whose dreams are operating here? What does the body language tell you?)

Statement: "I really don't care that much about what I'll get in algebra this semester. I've learned to take the pressure off myself."

The possible feeling(s) beneath the words:

CAUTION

DON'T IGNORE THOSE FEELINGS!

Here are six common ways that we unwittingly discount our children's feelings. Notice which ones sound most familiar to you:

- Denial: "How can you possibly be tired when you just had twelve hours' sleep?"
- Comparison: "Your friend Bobby isn't afraid of the water. What's _your_ problem?"
- Instruction: "You can't mean you hate the baby. You really love her."
- Ridicule: "What a wimp! Are you going to cry over a little scratch?"
- Threats: "If you're going to whine just because you weren't picked for the starting team, maybe you shouldn't be on the team at all."
- Sarcasm: "I just _love_ hearing about how much you hate my cooking in front of your grandmother!"[4]

(Hint: Discover whether your child has done something valuable [learned to take the pressure off] or is just making an excuse for a lack of effort. Look into it. For example, the teen could be saying, "This is too hard for me" or "Push me a little harder, please.")

Statement: Just before answering, Nikesha's eyes move upward and to the left, as if she's trying to look at something way up on the wall. Then she refocuses on you and says, "Mom, I'm telling you the truth—I was with my girlfriends all evening!"

The possible feeling(s) beneath the words:

(Hint: Most people have difficulty with eye contact when they're having a hard time with the truth. Does Nikesha fidget, too? Clear her throat? Start to sweat?)

Statement: Kara seems stiff and kind of "shut down." With little emotion, she says softly, "If you see any of my teammates in the next couple of days, will you just let 'em know how much I love them?"

The possible feeling(s) beneath the words:

(Hint: Warning! Warning! Take this comment seriously. Before attempting suicide, people try to tie up loose ends. Note: Teens have taken their own lives for reasons we would consider minor irritations—breaking up with a boyfriend, getting a failing grade, being called names at school.)

PLAYING FAIR ON THE FAMILY GRIDIRON

Have you considered how important trust is for a family? By the time children begin to play at a more competitive level, they will have discovered the sources of input they feel they can trust. If the parents haven't built a relationship of trust and understanding by that time, then they will soon find themselves out of the loop. But please understand that building a relationship of trust is not something you can just jump into at the last minute. It's something you establish over time, from the child's earliest years of involvement.

If you haven't done that, then you may find that you are constantly chasing your children, pursuing them, and trying to get them to open up to you. You may be saying, "Even though I didn't create a safe place for you to talk freely when you were younger, I really want to do that now." But sometimes, try as you will, it may be too late. Reaching out to them in this situation is still a risk, but it's important that we parents try to establish that kind of bond.

One of the best ways to lay a firm foundation of trust in your family is to determine that your family will always "fight fair." Now, as you probably know, any good book on communication will offer advice about fair fighting. I'm referring to techniques we can use to move through conflict rather than letting conflict deal a knockout blow to our relationships.

But let's have a little fun with this while making it sports-oriented too. Below, I've attached football penalty calls to some of the standard unfair fighting techniques. They point out some common ways we try to dodge our responsibility to communicate directly and take responsibility for our actions. Have you recognized any of these in your family? Take a moment to write down some notes about the last time you heard or used any of them. Then be sure to talk with other family members about these techniques. Plan to avoid any major penalties in the future! Here are my Seven Interpersonal Communication Penalty Situations:

1. Illegal Motion: This is a vague and tricky offensive infraction. Acting as though we're moving toward giving a direct, specific complaint, we then back up and offer a hard-to-nail-down accusation. Left unchecked, this tactic can dissolve into generalized whining. Example: "You don't need me to tell you how weird you've been acting. I'm sure you can figure out for yourself what's bothering me!"

How I've committed this penalty with my spouse or kids (describe what happened):

2. Unsportsmanlike Conduct: We've hurt somebody, and they've let us know it. But rather than responding with a sincere attempt to comfort, we hit back even harder. How? We pull out our own hurt as an example of even worse behavior by the other person. This tactic might also be called "dueling blockers," since our main goal is to push the other guy harder than he's pushing us and to show how much worse we've been treated. Example: "I know I hurt you, but just think how much it hurt me when you…"

How I've committed this penalty with my spouse or kids (describe what happened):

3. Ineligible Receiver: Here's where we insert ancient misdeeds into the conversation. These should have been cut from the family team and forgotten years ago. But we finally bring them in to make the most hurtful impact. They can be totally devastating. Example: "I haven't mentioned this in a long time, Bill, but since you are being so unreasonable, may I just remind you that back in 1973, the one thing you did was…"

How I've committed this penalty with my spouse or kids (describe what happened):

4. Piling On: This one's easy to understand. We just keep bringing up the faults and flaws of the other person until he's overwhelmed. Keep piling on the complaints until he's squashed! Example: "Oh yeah? Well you're not exactly the most polite. You never call when you're going to be late. You always forget to clean your room. You have bad breath a lot. You keep choosing crummy friends, and you…" Get the picture?

How I've committed this penalty with my spouse or kids (describe what happened):

5. Jumping Offsides: Here's where we make a huge leap from the specific to the universal. We do it when we generalize about someone's behavior based on a single, isolated action. The words "always" and "never" keep creeping into the conversation. Example: "You missed my game? You never come to my games! You're always too busy! You always ignore me. I can never count on you!"

How I've committed this penalty with my spouse or kids (describe what happened):

6. Late Hit: This is the unfair technique of applying guilt with passive-aggressive comments. It often involves sarcasm, which bubbles up near the end of an argument. Example: "Now that we've talked all about this, Sharon, I hope you're feeling 'comfortable' with what you chose to do. I know I'm just fine with it. And I'm sure the kids will think you're just great! Wow! What a great Mom!"

How I've committed this penalty with my spouse or kids (describe what happened):

7. Personal Foul: This basically involves "roughing the passer" by making a personal attack. Instead of sticking to the issues and solving the problem, we switch to manhandling the person. The term "character assassination" comes to mind. Example: "Bounced again? If only you weren't so bad at math, you'd be able to keep the checkbook balanced. You've never been very good with figures, have you?"

How I've committed this penalty with my spouse or kids (describe what happened):

KEEP IT TOGETHER DURING SPORTS CRISES

If your child is involved in any kind of sport for very long, you will have to deal with a crisis of some kind. It's inevitable. Sooner or later there will be a situation demanding a thoughtful response. Good communication can come to the rescue again!

My best advice is this: Don't wait until it happens to start thinking about how you'll deal with it. I believe the parents' role is to raise their child's self-esteem and to validate the child's sense of self-worth when circumstances might cause her to question those things. The parent can ensure that the child understands that her importance in the family is not conditional and is not affected by her performance in the sport, whether good or bad. The caring parent will say, "The world will always want you to perform, but we love you regardless of how you do on the field. That's not the important thing for us."

Let me illustrate. Our daughter Audra decided when she was in the fourth grade that she wanted to play the guitar, so she took lessons and progressed to playing fairly well. But she didn't always spend as much time as she needed to in rehearsing and preparing her lessons. At the end of the period it came time for her music recital. Again, she didn't spend as much time as she could have, and during the performance she barely made it through.

She made so many mistakes!

Janet and I were sitting there in pain, feeling just what she was going through. With all the mistakes she was making, we knew she must be terrified, but I immediately realized the courage she was showing, going up in front of all those people and not quitting when she wasn't doing very well. When she finally got through, she came running off stage and just fell into her mother's arms. Janet said, " Audra, Daddy and I are so proud of you for completing the whole thing. That took courage."

PARENTING POINT

A POSTGAME INTERACTION SEQUENCE
- Respond to the emotions with reflective statements only: "So you're feeling real low right now?"
- Let the child take the lead in conversation. Silence—lots of it—is okay.
- Wait until tomorrow to discuss strategy and/or instruction. If your child wants to watch your video of the game, fine. Just watch. Often he'll think, "I guess I did better than I thought."

Audra looked up with big tears in her eyes and she said, "Oh, Mommy, was it awful?" But Janet said, "No, Audra, we could see that you were working through it, and you made some mistakes, but you didn't stop. A lot of people would have stopped, but you didn't. You persevered, and I'm proud of you." Those words were like medicine to Audra. Suddenly she knew she was appreciated.

That wasn't the time to say, "Well, Audra, you see, that's what your father and I have been telling you! That's what happens when you don't practice enough!" We could make that point later, when she wasn't so vulnerable.

That little crisis taught some important lessons about how to prepare for all the other kinds of crises that regularly happen in a sports family. When kids are out there competing, they are going to hit the wall once in a while. When that happens, here's the basic approach I recommend:

1. When in crisis, first provide a safe place. Janet and I say that teaching always takes place in the context of life. But before teaching can take place, you have to deal with the emotion of the moment. When your child is in the throes of an emotional experience, that's not the time to teach them the fundamentals of the game. Instead, it's time to go home and offer anything that nurtures and comforts—food, massage, a warm bath, sitting by the fire, a quiet nap—anything but a critique!

2. When in crisis, separate the event from the relationship. Yes, you want your children to do well in their sport, and you expect them to show some self-discipline and concentration on the field, but that's not the only thing that concerns you. The most important thing is that you love your child, that you're proud for them to be getting this experience and exposure. You also realize that they're going to mess up sometimes. It happens. But you have to let them know that you will be there with open arms, regardless of their performance in any game on any day.

3. When in crisis, don't talk strategy. You'll find there are times when you can offer input, give a critique, or make constructive changes that will be well received by your children. But after an emotional game, when you're still feeling the sting of a big loss or a bad performance, that's not the time to start talking strategy. If somebody in your family dies, the last thing you want is for some well-meaning friend or relative to tell you, "You really need to read Psalm 23, my friend, and find a word of consolation." In moments of grief and loss, what you need is someone to grieve with you. Sometimes just being there, in silence, is the best gift you can offer. The time for analysis will come later, and anyone who is truly sensitive will know to give you some time and space to recover.

So remember that young athletes mostly need some kind of release after a big game. They need to blow off steam and relax, and that often means horsing around or just doing something silly. If parents try to capture that time and use it as a way to critique the game or to analyze the child's performance, then the parent is actually hurting more than helping. And who of us wants that?

DEVELOPING THE FAMILY GAME PLAN

STEP 9: STRIVE FOR THE HIGHEST LEVELS OF COMMUNICATION IN YOUR FAMILY.

As a family, talk together about which levels of communication you've reached in your family? Jot down some notes about how you can heighten the communication level when needed:

Which of the communication techniques in this chapter seem most helpful to you? Which do you need to work on in your family? Talk together about this.

Plan to tell another family member about one of your needs (of which they may not be aware). Use "I" statements, then wait for the other's response. Later, make some notes here about what happened. Also note how you might do this kind of sharing in a more effective way in the future.

PART FOUR

The Coach

Get to Know Me!

"Quit whining, Ted. Your role on this team is to stay on that bench and lend vocal support."

As you'd suspect, I was a pretty good player coming up as a youngster in baseball. But I had three bad experiences along the way. All of them involved coaches who made decisions about my playing time.

Decisions that thoroughly infuriated my dad.

Dad's overreacting and public venting just added to my pressures, though I got through it.

But does this have anything to do with you? I'm guessing it does. Because no matter how good your child is, I'm quite sure that one or both of you will eventually experience frustration or conflict with a coach, if you haven't already.

When that happens, your job is not to panic or run out on the field and get into a fight. (I know, you'd never do that anyway, right? But maybe your style would be to fume silently and badmouth the coach behind his back. Or perhaps you'd come up with some other creative way to fight.) Instead, your job is to think through those sticky coach-conflict events and attempt to learn from them.

A good place to start, even before there is a conflict, is to do some serious investigation by asking yourself, "How much do I know about coaches in general and about this coach in particular?" The more you know, the better off you'll be whenever you're tempted to butt heads with the local chief of the Pee Wee Titan Field Hockey Club. So I suggest that you sit back and consider three big questions about coaches and coaching. These should help you see how well you understand what it's like down in the team-leading trenches.

DO I KNOW HOW THE COACH SEES THINGS?

Calmly attempt to view things from the coach's perspective before reacting. I recall a situation with our son when he was in high school. He was the number-two pitcher on the team at the start of his senior year, playing behind Todd Van Poppel, a young man who would end up being a first-round draft pick. Aaron pitched the first two games of the season, but his team lost close, low-scoring games before another pitcher replaced him and kept Aaron's starting job the rest of the season. I was angry. I wanted to protect my child from hurt. I wanted to confront the coach. Thankfully, I was able to call upon my own experiences as a kid—when Dad occasionally would jump in the coach's face—to help me resist the temptation to blow up.

Later I surmised that the coach had made his decisions based purely on what he thought was in the best interest of the team. The school had a successful baseball program centered on outstanding talent and a reputation for winning. (They have turned out several kids who went on to the pros.) He just decided that Aaron wasn't going to be the player to get him to where he wanted to go. I now see that the decision was never personal but much more practical. Indeed, the team ended up going to the state championships that year on Van Poppel's shoulders.

I tell this story to make a crucial point: From the coach's perspective, what's best for the team takes precedence over player politics. Or to put it another way, winning—not politics—is uppermost in virtually every coach's mind. If we can keep this fact firmly planted in our minds, it will save us a lot of anguish. It also helps to remember that we parents often use the term "politics" to explain why our child isn't playing because we don't want to admit that he or she just isn't good enough at this point in time.

This sort of brings us full circle. Coaches aren't going to pull the players they feel can help them win games because, as you move up into the higher competition levels, the focus will be more and more on winning the game. The goal of winning is a reality that we must adjust to as we move through the sporting years, and we do our kids a disservice not to prepare them for that kind of world after they leave the nest. Competition and winning will be an everyday event in the marketplace. Similarly, the coach is going to make his or her decisions based on what's good for the team and its record. You, of course, will make your own decisions based on what's good for your child. That's just how it works; there's no use raging.

There is one more issue here, though, regarding your own internal conflict. Ultimately, parents want victories too. They'll say, "Put in the players who can help us win!" But when it comes to their child getting pulled from the game, suddenly there's a total disconnect. They don't know what to do. They express anger or frustration, or they may say things like, "Hey, that's not fair! It's political. You realize you're keeping my kid from getting a scholarship, don't you?"

We're not always objective in these situations. But again, I urge you to remember that, nine times out of ten, the coach's decisions on who to play and when have nothing to do with anything personal or political. We can always see everybody else's kid with 20/20 clarity. But when it comes to our own precious offspring, we grow pretty nearsighted.

STAY OR GO?
Coaches ask themselves: "How do I know I'm in the right place?" Here's
how those who stay typically answer:
- "I still have passion about what I'm doing."
- "I still have the ability to endure difficulties here without bitterness."
- "I still have more wins than losses!"
- "I still find contentment in this place, with these players and parents."

Frustrated parent, it's time for you to accept that politics just don't have much to do with coaching decisions. I sometimes hear parents say, "Hey, they're not fielding the best players." But most coaches roll their eyes when they hear something like that. It doesn't make much sense when you think about it. If his or her job depends on whether or not the team wins consistently and the only way that can happen is by using the best players, does anybody really think the coach is going to bench the best athletes just because of some grudge he or she may have against a player or parent? Not likely. It's not a matter of who the coach likes or dislikes. It's always a matter of which players can win the game for us.

Winning becomes more important for the players, too, as they grow older. It's a natural transition. But what we do have to watch out for is the coach whose total focus is on winning to the extent that he's threatening the dignity of the children. Some coaches would push seven- and eight-year-olds with the same intensity that they push sixteen- and seventeen-year-olds, and that's neither realistic nor fair.

Recently I heard about a lady who pulls her daughter out of one sports program after another because of her perception about her daughter's lack of playing time. The lady herself was joking that she was sewing together pieces of material from the girl's various uniforms and that just from this year alone she was going to have a large quilt! This lady was desperately trying to control her daughter's situation until she could find a place where she could play.

Instead of approaching the situation by trying a different sport or staying on a team long enough to get to know the other players and the coach, this mother pulled her little girl out of a league after just one game.

What was this mother teaching her child? At the first sign of conflict, you should jump ship and run. Do not commit to anything. If things don't go well for you right from the start, then take off and head in another direction.

Most of us know that anything of value takes time. It requires working hard, persevering through difficulty, and waiting for the day when it all starts to come together. It's painful for me to say this, but this young girl may never know what it takes to succeed in anything. She's being conditioned to avoid problems by running from them.

And one more thing: If you're around a sport long enough, you will observe major shifts in coaching plans from one year to the next. Coaches may say they're going to run a certain type of offense this year, but run it the opposite way next year. They may say they only want a 5-foot-10-inch setter on the volleyball team this year, and then two years down the road they'll want a 5-foot-7-inch setter. We need to expect this, not fight it!

When I was coming up in sports, the scouts were continually telling my father that, at 5-foot-10, I was too short to be a Major League catcher. Nevertheless, I continued to play my game the best way I could, and before long the coaches were saying I was exactly the right size for the job!

Things change. People change. Strategies change. If you expect it, you can help your child to anticipate and deal with the circumstances that will arise. You may say, "This is how it looks right now. At this moment, you don't have a place on the team. They're going to use somebody else, but that can change." You want to tell her to keep her cool and not to show any frustration, but stay tuned in. Stay in shape and be ready for what may come next.

If your child has a good attitude and a sense of expectancy, good things can still happen. Things will change. But even if they don't change dramatically, it's important to stay calm and optimistic about her chances down the road. Coaches in the more competitive programs already envision what kind of team they're looking for, regardless of who shows up for tryouts. They know the positions they want to fill and what skills those players must have. If you understand this in advance, it can help you head off some potential conflict.

Finally, never forget that coaching is a tough job! At least, that's how most coaches themselves see it. Just listen to some of the most successful ones.[1]

The reason I resigned at this time is because the duties and the pressures of this position have begun to make me into something that I don't want to be.

—DAN ISSEL

FORMER HEAD COACH OF THE DENVER NUGGETS

Sometimes being a coach is like being a second lieutenant in a combat zone. Eventually you are going to get shot.

—LARRY BROWN

ANNOUNCING HIS RESIGNATION FROM THE INDIANA PACERS

I tell guys, if I don't yell at you once in a while, forget about it, I'm not really interested in you. I've got to get inside and make you realize how good you can be.

—JOE PATERNO

HEAD COACH, PENNSYLVANIA STATE UNIVERSITY

In its native state it's nothing, but in its final, polished state it's beautiful. How do you refine it and get it to the final stage? You put it under heat, fire, pressure.

—MIKE DITKA

ON WHY A PLAYER IS LIKE A DIAMOND

LET'S GET TOGETHER

If you're a coach, be sure to schedule a coach-parent meeting each season. You'll improve the parents' understanding of youth sports and what you are trying to accomplish. Here are some specific purposes for your meeting:

- To enable parents to become acquainted with you.
- To educate parents about the objectives of youth sports and clarify the goals of your program.
- To inform parents about the specifics of the program and what is expected of the children and parents relative to these details. This includes obtaining parental assistance for accomplishing various tasks and conducting the season's activities.
- To get parents to understand and reinforce the positive approach to coaching that you will be using.
- To inform parents about their youth sport obligations and commitments.
- To establish clear lines of communication between you and parents.
- To help you understand the concerns of parents.[2]

We don't just play football around here. We learn how to become grown-ups, how to mature, how to become men.

—NEBRASKA QUARTERBACK SCOTT FROST

ON PLAYING FOR TOM OSBORNE

To those thousands of alumni sitting up in stands, players are numbers. They're a big old helmet, with a big old shoulder pad, with a 12 number down there. It's a hero type of thing. They don't see the inside of them like we do. We know these kids— they're like our children. We don't want to see them fail. So, a lot of times, we want to give them a second chance.

—BOBBY BOWDEN

HEAD COACH, FLORIDA STATE UNIVERSITY

You go in a corner, you get a glass of milk, you suck on your thumb
and you let somebody else make the decisions.

—JERRY GLANVILLE

ON HOW YOU'D COACH IF YOU WANTED PEOPLE TO LIKE YOU

Sound like it's easy to be a coach?

DO I KNOW WHAT TO LOOK FOR IN A GOOD COACH?
Listen to retired Oakland Raider Howie Long, speaking about former coach
Al Davis on ESPN's *Sunday Conversation* in 1994: "The ironic thing is that
I've never seen him and Darth Vader in the same place."

Sounds pretty sinister, doesn't it? Even with tongue in cheek, we still
have to admit the existence of a few bad coaches out there. So right up front,
let me say this: If you see your child being badgered by a coach, then you
may need to pull your child out of the program. It's paramount, particularly
before your child reaches age eleven, that you monitor the level of play, the
type of coaching, and who you let into the child-mentoring role. Once
little Timmy finally enters junior-high sports, you can generally release him
a little more; just be there to help him through the rough spots on a case-by-
case basis.

In the teen years the child's level of maturity should be great enough
that you can talk to her about a ranting coach and teach her some strategies
for dealing with these kinds of stresses. Overriding all this, of course, is your
own adult perspective and protective instincts. If you find that your child's
coach is always yelling at the kids or is constantly screaming obscenities,
then you may need to take a more proactive approach by removing your
child from the program. You may even need to meet the organization lead-
ers, who can deal more directly with the problem by speaking to the coach.
Parents don't have to put up with all the things that coaches say and do,
especially when it involves kids at the younger ages.

Part of our parental responsibility is to act as a filter to evaluate the people who come into our child's life. Whether coaches, teachers, other parents, other players, or anyone else, people who are negative or angry or vulgar should not be allowed in. During the child's early years, the parent is the only one with the maturity to exercise discretion in these areas.

At this point, you may be wondering, "So how can I tell when I have a good coach working with my kids?" I'd suggest you look for things like these characteristics.

A GOOD COACH IS HONEST AND CONSISTENT.

Whether you like it or not, a coach who tells you the truth and doesn't abuse your trust will be a feather in your cap. Once that trust is broken, though—with the very first instance—you must be willing to confront. Maybe the

CAUTION

ARE YOU LEGAL?
An increasing number of lawsuits have been filed against youth sport coaches, and the court decisions in these cases have established the legal responsibilities of coaches. If you are a coach, your awareness of these responsibilities can...enhance the welfare of young athletes—as well as your ability to defend yourself against litigation!
- Provide a safe physical environment.
- Provide proper and safe equipment.
- Plan the activity properly.
- Provide safe and proper instruction.
- Provide close supervision.
- Warn athletes and parents of inherent risks.
- Match athletes on physical size and skill attributes.
- Evaluate athletes for injury, illness, or incapacity.
- Provide adequate medical assistance.
- Keep adequate records.
- Obtain liability insurance.[3]

coach forgot a promise she made; maybe she just didn't realize anyone was listening. But in any event, it's up to you to encourage the highest standards of integrity. The kids are watching!

Along with this goes a predictable consistency. It always helps to relieve tension when we know how the coach will approach the season, apply a policy, and set the rules. We don't expect strategies to remain set in stone, as I mentioned above. But we do expect, in the realm of team discipline, rules, and policies, that all will be consistently applied without favoritism or constant "exceptions." Again, watch the actions of the coach—not just what he says.

A GOOD COACH IS SUPPORTIVE.

There's nothing better than a coach who works to keep kids feeling like a part of the team, even if they're not playing much. Coaches who think intimidation is motivation offer no support at all.

It can also be hurtful to have a coach, especially in the early years, who is overly critical or who puts the child under too much pressure. Parents need to give this a lot of thought: What kind of coach do I want my kids to be around in school, in select sports, in the community leagues? They need to ask, "Is this too much pressure from the coach? Is it hurrying my child too much psychologically, emotionally, or physically? Where is the support?"

A GOOD COACH IS A FINE TEACHER.

You can tolerate some verbal aggressiveness from a coach if he or she is a good teacher. Remember that actions speak louder than words.

Remember, too, that children's personalities determine how they adapt to a coaching style. Our three children were all different in this area. Aaron, our eldest, tended to be more reflective, conscientious, and creative. Briana, the youngest, is socially active, strong-willed, and spontaneous. Audra, our middle child, is goal-oriented, organized, and persevering. We have seen the whole range of emotions in our three kids, and we have had to learn a

"Sorry to disturb you, sir, but coach is wondering if it is OK to put you in the game."

much broader vocabulary in order to relate to each of them lovingly and intelligently.

We found that we had to be proactive in some areas, such as letting the coaches know what kind of children our kids were when they were first getting involved. For example, we might say, "If you yell, she's not going to understand that and she's very likely to get upset and cry." But for another, we might say, "You'll have to yell or do something visible to get her attention sometimes, just to let her know that you really mean business." In the early years, that kind of input can help a coach to work more effectively with your child.

A GOOD COACH LEAVES ROOM FOR PLAYER CREATIVITY.

I played for sixteen managers in sixteen years in baseball, and my favorite coaches were those who understood who I was and what I could do for the team. The best coach I ever worked for understood me, but he also understood that he might not know all there was to know about my potential. He left room in his perception of me for something else that he might not have anticipated.

He would say, in effect, "I'm leaving room for you to be more than I anticipate you being." He would say, "Here's what I want you to do, and I believe you have the ability to get it done. But, you know, you may have some skills that go beyond what I know and I want to leave that area open for you."

A GOOD COACH IS DISCIPLINED.

There's nothing worse than playing on or against a team that is unruly and disrespectful to others. 'Nuff said!

DO I KNOW HOW TO RESOLVE CONFLICTS WITH THE COACH?

I came across a newspaper column written by a Dr. Wallace who answers readers' questions on various aspects of child development and parenting. A father wrote in from Oakland, California, asking about his bench-riding son:

Dear Dr. Wallace:

My son is on the football team, but he rarely gets into a game. Last Friday night his team was leading 40 to 6 late in the fourth quarter, and my son still didn't get into the game. I'll admit he isn't a star player, but he makes good grades, obeys the team rules, and attends all the practices, even during the summer. John is in eleventh grade, and this is his third year of football.

PARENTING POINT

TOO MUCH BENCH TIME?
When your child isn't playing, encourage her to:
- Work diligently on skill improvement.
- Stay in shape.
- Be ready to play.
- Keep a friendly, positive attitude.

I'm not a pushy parent and never will be, but I don't see why the coach can't play my son and the other "scrubs" for a few downs after the win or loss is no longer in doubt. I'd like your thoughts on this.

Take a moment to stop and think. How would you have answered this father? Here was a part of Dr. Wallace's reply, in the form of a personal anecdote:

Dear Father:

When I was coaching basketball at LaQuinta High School in Garden Grove, California, we had the ball with a five-point lead and were stalling, trying to run out the clock. Then one of our players was fouled with one second left on the clock. I called time out and immediately inserted four players who didn't get much playing time.

The shooter missed the free throw and the ball came to one of our scrubs, who batted the ball toward the hoop and, wouldn't you know, it went in as the horn sounded. Dwight Fichtner scored two points playing one second. He was thrilled, his parents were thrilled, and I was very happy for Dwight. After the game, I told him that if he could score at that rate for an entire game, he'd average 3,840 points per game![4]

I like this Dr. Wallace. I think he has a realistic picture of the coach's needs and the team's needs. A high-school coach must get the win first. Then comes making a "scrub" player feel absolutely great. If we were talking about a younger age group, I'd want a different reply. I'd want all the little athletes to have a crack at playing in each game.

But this young football player, at his age, must now learn to get what he can from his sports experience, whether or not he ever achieves much playing time. He can work hard over the summer, of course, and hope to play more in his senior year. He can enjoy friendships on the team and offer his help and support in creative ways along the sidelines and off the field. Or he can say: "Football is not my forte; maybe I'll try track and field—or get a job or work on my studies or find a new hobby." Any of these options would be just fine. But let's not come down on a high-school coach who's just trying to win games with the best he's got.

Now all of this brings me to something quite practical that we can add to our question about conflict. I encourage you to head toward three specific goals when dealing with coaches and conflicts:

FIRST GOAL: BECOME COMFORTABLE IN TRANSFERRING RESPONSIBILITY FOR CONFLICT RESOLUTION TO YOUR CHILD.

As I've said from the start, the most important things that happen through sports in the early years are developing character, honing basic skills, and learning to have fun. But at some point we parents need to prepare our child for the coach's more aggressive approach to winning. We may need to say, "Johnny, we've let you play, we've watched you have fun, and we've wanted you to have a good foundation in sports. Your teams have won in certain situations and they've lost in others, but from this point on you're going to be playing for coaches whose reputations depend on their ability to win. Winning is going to be a lot more important this year."

A natural transition takes place in the parent-child relationship when the parent starts doing less to teach and defend the child and the child begins to take on more of the responsibility. This transition usually takes place somewhere around the beginning of the high-school years. That's when you'll begin to see the child assuming more of the decision-making process and, simultaneously, the parent is guiding the child into shouldering more of the responsibility for dealing directly with his or her frustration, disappointment, and conflicts.

If you go about it in the right way, eventually your child will reach the point where he can handle his own relational issues on a day-to-day basis. Our daughter Briana came home one day after having a meeting with her coach, and she said, "I just started crying like a baby." Janet said, "Well, that's normal, Briana. You'll get better at managing those emotions the more you dialogue in situations like this. Emotional situations like that sometimes bring out your deepest feelings." Going in and talking to authority figures is something we all have to learn how to do, because we will be doing it, one way or another, for the rest of our lives.

Then Janet and I said, "Okay, we know how you feel, and we want you to understand that we're behind you all the way. But we're not getting into this situation. We'll help you think it through, so you'll have some idea how to approach the coach. But then you need to go in and talk it out for yourself." Seeing my child pluck up her courage and do this was healing for me, too. Most of the time, my dad would go in and fight my battles with coaches for me, and I saw how damaging that could be. Now I saw myself paving the way for a different result. (The only way either of us, as parents, would go in to deal with a coach was if the coach had done something that was extremely destructive in some way. There were a few times when one of us would go in and say, "Coach, you mishandled this," and we would deal with that.)

What can a player say? Well, she might go in and say, "Coach, I've noticed that in the last couple of games my standing has slipped. Is there some part of my game that I can work on to help me get back into the mix of things?" What the player is doing with that statement is, first of all, getting some information. The coach may say, "No, you haven't slipped. I just need to take a look at this new player right now. I need to see how this person can contribute to the team, so that's why I've put her in your spot." In that case your child has learned something about the team strategy. That's helpful! The new information will probably also help you, the parent, alleviate some confusion and frustration.

On the other hand, the coach may say, "Yes, thanks for asking. Here are some things you need to work on." She'll offer advice about some areas where your child's game needs to improve. Or she may share the plan for how she's thinking of using her, or talk about the role she has in mind for her in the big picture of the entire season.

I tell kids that the question, "Why are you doing this to me?" is potentially very dangerous, so avoid it. But asking for pointers on how you can improve your game gives the coach a chance to offer constructive advice and input. What you're saying in that case is, "What can I do as a player to improve my position?" and the coach will see that. This shows a much better attitude, and along the way you may gain some good, practical insights about your skills.

These are some of the ways players themselves can take charge when they're angry about a coaching decision. But when the parent is the only advocate, doing all the talking, kids grow up feeling that they have no control over the situation or even their own destiny. It's no wonder some kids feel lost when they get to college and have to talk to a professor or meet new people! They've always had everything handled for them, and they don't know how to initiate a meaningful conversation. If we want our children to be able to converse at an adult level, we need to help them start the process. What better way than to encourage them to go to their coach and talk it through? Obviously, this will be easier for some kids than others. At the appropriate age, though, they all need to gain the confidence to do it for themselves.

THIRD GOAL: ALL OF YOU WORK TO BECOME MORE COMFORTABLE ASKING OTHERS FOR HELP.

Parents, learn to ask others who have been there. Wondering how to relate to the varsity coach next year? Ask a few parents of varsity players this year.

Make the first move! You'll probably make some new friends, too.

At some point you'll find yourself in a situation where you've never been before and you're completely in the dark about how to handle it. The smart move is to start looking around for someone with the experience to guide you. Think: *Who do I know with some experience in this area? Who can give me an objective opinion on what's going on here?* More than likely it's not going to be someone in the organization or someone who has a vested interest in what happens out on the field. It needs to be someone with enough physical and emotional distance to give a good, solid, and fair reading of the situation. You can ask, "Did you ever run across this problem? How did you cope with it?" You can certainly learn from what you find out, and in some cases you may even ask this person to talk to your child as a mentor.

Now a final word of encouragement to you, my fellow parent: Never forget that winning at sports parenting is inevitable as long as you keep your child's best interests at heart. In spite of all the expert advice and proven techniques that still remain to be mastered, I'm convinced that our natural desire to bless our youngsters will carry us through, by God's grace. In other words, you just keep loving that child! As you learn to enjoy sports with him or her, I'm sure you'll find, as we have in our family, that the deepening of the relationships—and the plain old fun!—make enduring the occasional nicks and bruises of conflict well worth the trouble.

DEVELOPING THE FAMILY GAME PLAN

STEP 10: IN COACH-CONFLICT SITUATIONS, FIRST PULL BACK SO YOU CAN VIEW THINGS THROUGH THE COACH'S EYES.

When was the last time you felt frustrated or angry about a coach's decisions, attitudes, or strategies? What did you do?

Imagine being your child's coach for a moment…
    What pressures are you feeling?

What sense do you have of support from the parents?

What attitudes from the parents and the players do you most appreciate?

What things, coming from the parents, would help you the most? the least?

How have you helped your child(ren) learn to relate to coaches? What are some next steps you can take to help your child grow more confident about this?

Time-Out for Questions

"Aaaah! I've lost all signs of brain activity! Turn off the Dick Vitale basketball commentary!"

Parents are always asking me questions as I travel the country with our seminars and workshops. Maybe you have some questions too? If so, take a time-out with me. You'll no doubt find a few answers within this sampling of inquiries that have come from parents just like you:

Q: Jim, sports are very important for two of my kids. But my third child, the middle daughter, has other interests. The problem is that we seem to get so excited in our family about the games, seemingly leaving one child out of all the fun. Your advice?

I always say, beware of neglecting the nonsports members of your family! In the June 1999 feature on sports in *Time* magazine, the writers talked about people who were picking up and moving or doing other things on a grand scale because the total focus of the family was on one athletically talented child. In cases like that, it becomes apparent that the interests of the nonsports members of the family are being generally neglected. But just as no one person is more important than another on a team, the members of the family are all important and need to be treated with mutual respect. So make a real effort to pay attention to—and participate in—the interests of your daughter. Go to the art shows, attend the concerts, see the plays. Show no favoritism in your family!

Q: What if my good player plays on a "bad" team?

It's much easier to play on a good team than a bad one, of course. Playing on a bad team puts a lot more pressure on the good players. On a good team the responsibility is equalized, but when you don't have the same caliber of talent in all positions, then that increases the pressure on the good players who will feel a responsibility to try to carry the team through.

The most important thing for you to do is to discuss these issues with your child. Help him or her realize that sometimes teams go through losing seasons. That should not keep her from setting personal goals in skill development, leadership abilities, and attitudinal growth. Losing, after all, provides a great context in which to learn patience, perseverance, and conflict-resolution skills.

Q: I never played in organized sports, but I have a little boy who's just itching to get involved. I have no idea how to guide him. What do I do?

Have a little faith in the coach and you'll do fine. Find out when the coach's introductory meeting is and be sure to attend. Also try to attend every parent meeting you can. You may also enjoy volunteering for one of the activities that need to be accomplished on the periphery of a team (helping with the field, refreshments, transportation, etc.). Remember: You do not have to be an expert in your child's sport in order to be a supportive parent.

If you're still feeling a bit helpless as your child grows older, consider finding a mentor in the particular sport your boy's playing. Sometimes the best thing a parent can do is to tell the child, "I don't understand all this myself, but I'll try to find someone who knows more about it and see if they can't give you some good advice."

What you may need is someone to show you the ropes. Most coaches will tell you that there's really no such thing as an objective parent when it comes to "coaching" their own child. So a smart parent may have to look elsewhere for objective input.

Q: I'm a coach who has a child with a behavioral problem on the team. How do you handle that problem, Jim?

First, be sure it's actually a behavioral problem and not just immaturity or poor play. But if it is, indeed, a kid acting out, then I try to change the environment itself in some way to take away the potential for conflict: Move him to another position. Keep him out of certain game situations. You decide.

If that doesn't work, I'll bring the peer pressure of the team into play— but without singling out the particular player. We had a boy in baseball camp last summer who twice lost his temper. When I saw what was happening, I tried to observe what was going on in that situation and defuse it before it got any worse. But then, after the second time the same thing happened, I came to the whole group and said, "Guys, I want you be aware that there have been some things going on out there that can't continue to happen. There have been some players who have lost their temper, and we're not going to do that again. Here's what will happen if you do this: First, you won't be playing the game because you'll be sitting on the bench. Second, you won't be getting the baseball cards that we give out as rewards for those who do certain things well."

The coaches and I have found that these kids respond to rewards, and they really love baseball cards. So instead of making it a punishment when we have to correct a child, we start by withholding things they enjoy. Again, I try never to single out a player in front of the group. If it turns out that repeated warnings don't solve the problem, then you'll have to sit down with the kid and his parent and talk it through in private. But that's the choice of last resort.

Q: My child doesn't seem to realize that he's just not very good at his sport. Do I talk to him about this?

Kids do realize their weaknesses, no matter what you think. Your job is to encourage the child's strengths. Janet would say to our daughter, for example, "Briana, you're strength is not in English, but I know you can put sentences together. You can learn to do that because you do it every day when you talk to people. You may not want to become a great writer, but when you get to college you're going to have to write papers. So now is a good time to start preparing yourself."

The point is to give the child an honest assessment, an evaluation of the options, and then some practical motivation to do the best she can in areas she enjoys. Usually, after a period of time not doing well in a sport, the child herself will decide to drop out. Just let that happen. If she perseveres, then play up the things one can learn by being the best "bench player" possible. That can involve setting a personal goal of being a tough competitor against the starters during practice sessions. Along these lines, rent the video *Rudy*.

Q: My varsity player dropped a fly ball that would have been the final out. Two runs score; game over. What do you do when your kid makes a game-losing error for the hometown team?

So your kid really messed up and made a serious blunder on the field? First, step back and think. Ever seen a big-leaguer bounce one off his head? Then my suggestion is to wait until tomorrow for any meaningful conversation. The child needs time to feel bad, to cry, to be disappointed. Give him plenty of room for that. Hold back, listen, touch, reflect back all the pain-filled comments, but don't offer criticism or advice.

If he wants to talk in the morning, then spend most of your time listening to his disappointment and awfulizing: "I'll never play again. Coach hates me. I can't face them…" Do not try to change his feelings; instead, affirm those feelings. It is thoroughly appropriate for a human being to feel bad after making a mistake. This is a time to help your child learn how to move through grief—a very useful adult skill, since we require it any time we lose something of value to us.

Down the road, if you feel it's okay to make some kind of comment, then make your teaching points in the context of something positive. For a younger player, you might say: "Billy, I saw that you did a good job of X, Y, and Z that time. That was great. About this other thing, when that ball got by you, next time you might try it this way." Or maybe the coach can help with that skill in practice. My own preference is not to tell them they did it wrong but to show them how to do it right. "Look, Billy. Watch this. Here's the way this should look." And don't forget the role that your facial expressions and the tone of your voice play in all of this.

Q: Why are some children so much better at sports than others?

I've found several reasons for this. Among them are having brothers and sisters who paved the way, in terms of modeling interest and dedication; having a parent who encouraged lots of informal practice in the backyard; living in a neighborhood where sports are big with the kids on the block; and—the most important by far—natural, inborn talent.

Remember though, to distinguish between natural coordination (or supposed lack of it) and your child's level of maturation. You may think you have an uncoordinated kid, whereas, once she moves through a particular developmental event (or growth spurt) her coordination may kick in big time.

Q: I'm in the unenviable position of having to coach my own child. Any pointers, Jim?

The key is for both of you to understand that you'll be a coach on the field and a parent at home. Make sure this is crystal clear for both of you, and repeat the principle often. Demonstrate it well. Your child will have to realize that you'll be a split personality in this sense. She should become more and more comfortable with the idea that your role will change once you both hit the field. Do plenty of talking about your need to be objective about the skills and playing time of all the players, including her. Assure her that you will avoid favoritism (or overcompensating to show your child *less* favor than other players). You do have a responsibility to all the athletes on the team, not just your child. Let that be clear!

Q: You and Janet speak quite a bit about unconditional love. How do I know when I'm showing this kind of love?

It's probably simpler than you think! For example, "Nice play," "Good catch," "Great swing" and "Good try" are all words of unconditional positive regard.

Let me offer an example. Maybe you remember the story of Derek Redmond, the British runner who participated in the 400-meter event in the 1990 Olympics. Redmond was the outstanding runner in the field, and everyone expected him to win the gold medal that year. But about halfway around the track during the semifinals, Redmond pulled up suddenly and fell to the ground with a torn hamstring muscle. The crowd was stunned, and there was an audible gasp of shock and surprise. But as the fans looked on, the young man struggled to his feet and began to limp in obvious pain toward the finish line.

Then something happened. An older man came out of the stands and moved quickly toward the runner. Guards came forward, but others stopped them. It was Redmond's father coming down to help his son off the track. He reached out to Derek, but the athlete shook his head. He wasn't leaving until he finished the race. So the older man put his arm around his son, and together they limped to the finish line amidst a deafening ovation from the crowd.

Q: I'm always asking so many questions about the game that my son gets irritated. I'm sure I'm asking all the wrong questions—about how he performed, what the coach said, why certain things were done, etc. What questions should we ask after the game?

How about making space for your child to talk about what he or she experienced, while staying away from performance-based questions? How about:

- Did you have fun today? Tell me about it…
- How did you feel about your playing today?
- Did you achieve your goals today? Which ones?
- What things did you most enjoy about this game?

Q: My husband, "Brad," seems to be trying to make an athlete out of our son, "Jarod," who shows little interest on his own. Brad says Jarod will learn to like sports if he's given a chance to find out what it's like, thus requiring all the practice sessions. What do you say?

Your husband needs to realize that he can't make your child an athlete. If your boy is going to be one, it will be because of the skills and strengths and motivations that are already within him. If he happens to achieve success in a competitive environment, you should be proud, and yes, you did contribute to it by parenting the child. But athletic ability is a matter of instinct and nature and a lot of other things that can't be forced. If those things aren't there naturally, you can't make the child a star, no matter how hard you try.

Additionally, if the child comes to feel that the success or failure of the family depends on his being a good athlete, he can become driven by emotions and be crippled by a fear of failure. A lot of fantastic players never make it to the pros because, somewhere along the way, they crumbled under those kinds of pressures. And some who do make it aren't all that emotionally stable after they arrive. We recently heard about a high-school quarterback who gets so upset before a game that he always throws up. Amazingly, there are some adults who think that's cute.

Q: You talk about "providing a safe place" as a primary duty of parents. Would you expand on that?

I believe there are four basic duties of parents: (1) helping our children find their calling; (2) setting them free emotionally; (3) encouraging the development of safe relationships; and (4) providing a home that is a safe place. What these duties entail are support, encouragement, involvement, and security. Every child needs those four things.

The safe place is where they will feel protected and loved. If that safe place is not the child's home, then where else would it be? A safe place is more than just the child's room, though! Children need the family to be their safe place during the important growing-up years. It's safe when they can talk about anything on their mind without censure (though they can expect wise parental judgment and critique); when they can be as emotional as they need to be without being destructive (though they can expect the requirement of respecting others in the family); and when they can make their own decisions about the level of sports involvement they would enjoy.

Q: I know I'm probably overprotective. But I just don't want my son to have to face conflict or other negative experiences, because I can't stand to see him hurt. Isn't it okay for me to pave the way for him when things go wrong?

Sometimes parents feel so strongly about giving their children security that they may inhibit natural development to the degree that the child never becomes self-sufficient. Their individuality and self-confidence have been compromised.

Maybe this will help you. I remember speaking in a minimum-security prison to a group of young offenders in my home state of Illinois, and I didn't meet a single kid who would admit that he had done anything wrong. The most common attitude was that they were victims. Somebody else was to blame for their being incarcerated. The authorities told me that because of their attitudes, more than 80 percent of those kids would spend the rest of their lives in and out of confinement because they couldn't deal with the idea of accountability and responsibility.

I'm not trying to scare you, but realize that your child must come to recognize the importance of being accountable for his own behavior. In adult life we are going to run up against hurt. We should teach our children about responsibility for their own behavior from the earliest years, even when it means watching them endure some pain. You teach them that they have the power to set a direction so that when bad things happen, and they will, they can step up to the plate and do the right thing. Yes, you want them to avoid situations that can get them into hot water. But you also want them to have the character to accept responsibility for their own mistakes and to deal with the consequences.

Q: What do I do after I've already blown it with my child by yelling or coming out with a hurtful comment?

Just apologize! If a parent accidentally steps over the line and says something that is hurtful, then he or she can come to the child and say, "I'm really sorry about what I said. I handled that all wrong, and I shouldn't have said it. Will you forgive me?" That has a tremendous impact on the child. Your son or daughter has a chance to learn some important lessons from your example at an early age. We don't do that often enough, I'm afraid. Maybe it's because we see it so seldom in other areas of our lives.

Q: I have a child who is very talented athletically. But it seems to be going to his head. What do you recommend?

Have a little talk with him about his Creator! A spiritual viewpoint can really help here. If your son begins to realize that his athletic ability is a gift from God, then he can celebrate it without undue pride or arrogance. You may say, "Isn't it neat that God saw fit to trust you with this talent, which has been your blessing all these years?" And if he can give God the credit for his gift, he'll grow in respect for the gifts and talents of others too. This perspective takes all of the "I'm better than you!" off the field.

We see a lot of professional athletes these days who have discovered this fact. You will see players in Major League Baseball, the National Football League, and the National Basketball Association stopping to pray together before or after the game, to say something to the media announcers about their faith, or to point up to the One who helped them make a special play. That's not grandstanding; it's the effort of men who've discovered that pride and arrogance are potentially self-destructive. They've simply chosen to give credit to the One who put them where they are.

Q: You briefly mentioned the concept of blessing our children. What do you mean?

It's an old-fashioned idea that seems more important today than ever. For me, it goes back to the Old Testament. You may remember the story of Jacob and Esau struggling to get the blessing of their father, Isaac. It's interesting that Esau was willing to give up his birthright but not his blessing. The blessing was the most important thing to him.

Janet and I recently participated in our son's wedding, and we arranged to make the rehearsal dinner a time of blessing. In our little ceremony, I blessed the couple in a number of ways and assured them that we, as their family, would always be there for them. In their book *The Blessing,* Gary Smalley and John Trent list several steps you can take to make this a very dynamic process. Please read this book!

Q: You've spoken of developing a family mission statement. Could you be more specific?

First, determine to develop a mission statement for your own life. For me, it's been something that I'm able to reflect on whenever I need to regroup or to take stock of what I'm doing at any given moment. It gives me a constant reminder of the big picture and always leads me to a better perspective on each day, and it helps me to express my purpose. Basically, I took

James Dobson's statement and adapted it to my situation. My mission statement says: "I have concluded that all the accumulation of wealth, even if I could achieve it, is an insufficient reason for living. When I reach the end of my days, I must look backward on something more than just Gold Glove awards, all-star games, world championships, and records; nor is fame of any lasting benefit. I will consider my earthly existence to have been wasted unless I recall a loving family, a consistent investment in the lives of people, and an earnest attempt to serve the God who made me."

Now, for the family to develop a mission statement, you'll need to plan several meetings together. Give everyone a chance to talk about their joys, fears, goals, dreams, and visions for family life. In this context of brainstorming, write down responses where everyone can see. Work on developing two or three sentences that sum up for you all what your family stands for and how it expects to operate in the future. Every family statement will be unique, so don't think there are any right or wrong ways to do it. Just be sure that you refer to it regularly, especially when entering conflict or dealing with practical problem solving. Your overall principles of family living and your general goals should guide you as you enter specific situations.

Q: How can I tell when my child is under too much stress?

Look for the standard symptoms! Psychologist Antoinette Saunders in her book *The Stress-Proof Child* lists a number of things you may observe:

- unexplained aching muscles
- neckaches
- backaches
- pounding heart
- frequent headaches
- restlessness
- impulsive, uncontrolled eating
- difficulty concentrating
- difficulty sleeping
- difficulty staying awake
- unexplained tiredness
- chronic irritability
- irritating behavior
- lack of naturalness and spontaneity
- nail biting, hair pulling, other nervous habits
- habitual picking at sores or scabs

When you see several of these symptoms in your child, and they don't go away after a period of time, then it's time to explore what's happening inside. Make safe spaces to let feelings come through. Offer to talk. You may both decide to change some situational things that would relieve the pressure. You may talk with teachers and coaches to make adjustments in the child's schedule. If you sense serious problems that keep your child depressed or anxious, consider entering family therapy together.

Q: Is there much difference in dealing with boys and dealing with girls in sports?

Yes! The key is to know that boys and girls differ greatly in emotional expression. There's a cultural difference between boys and girls in this regard. Boys can be sensitive about their feelings up to the age of about twelve or thirteen and get away with it, but if they react emotionally or cry when their feelings are hurt beyond that point, they'll often be ridiculed and teased. In fact, some parents will notice an emotional reaction in their son and say, "Okay, stop acting like a baby!" But the most serious teasing usually comes from their peers. So boys learn very quickly to mask these feelings.

Girls have a little more freedom to express their emotions. Janet and I see this quite a bit when we go to Briana's volleyball tournaments. If her team loses a big game, the girls will cry. And if they win a big game, sometimes they cry too! It's a little easier for girls. Society expects them to be more emotional, even though no psychologist would tell you that the emotions men feel are that much different from what women feel.

The Game-Plan Steps, Summarized

DEVELOPING YOUR FAMILY GAME PLAN

Step 1: Begin monitoring the level of sports tension in your family.

Step 2: Seriously plan for fun.

Step 3: Begin assessing the motivational makeup of your child(ren).

Step 4: Determine to focus on character development, win or lose.

Step 5: Check to make sure that the best life lessons are hitting home with your kids.

Step 6: Be sure you are getting your own needs met so you can best meet the needs of your child.

Step 7: Determine your basic game-day personality and work on turning its weaknesses into strengths.

Step 8: Don't assume; find out what your children actually want.

Step 9: Strive for the highest levels of communication in your family.

Step 10: In coach-conflict situations, first pull back so you can view things through the coach's eyes.

Some Resources, for Your Information

RECOMMENDED READING LIST

Burnett, Darrell. *Youth Sports and Self-Esteem: A Guide for Parents.* Indianapolis: Masters Press, 1993.

Campbell, D. Ross. *How to Really Love Your Child.* Wheaton, Ill.: Victor Books, 1980.

Cline, Foster, and Jim Fay. *Parenting Teens with Love and Logic.* Colorado Springs: Pinon Press, 1992.

Hohenstein, Kurt. *The Rules of the Game: Simple Truths Learned from Little League.* Nashville: Nelson, 1996.

Lewis, Paul. *Five Key Habits of Smart Dads.* Grand Rapids: Zondervan, 1994.

McPherson, Miles. *The Power of Believing in Your Child.* Minneapolis: Bethany, 1998.

Micheli, Lyle. *Sportswise: An Essential Guide for Young Athletes, Parents, and Coaches.* Boston: Houghton Mifflin, 1990.

Rosemond, John. *Teen-Proofing: A Revolutionary Approach to Fostering Responsible Decision Making in Your Teenager.* Kansas City: Andrews McMeel, 1998.

Ryan, Joan. *Little Girls in Pretty Boxes: The Making and Breaking of Elite Gymnasts and Figure Skaters.* New York: Warner Books, 1995.

Sanders, Summer. *Champions Are Raised, Not Born: How My Parents Made Me a Success.* New York: Delacorte Press, 1999.

Saunders, Antoinette, and Bonnie Remsberg. *The Stress-Proof Child.* New York: Holt, Rinehart and Winston, 1984.

Simmons, Dave. *Dad the Family Coach: How to Build Teamwork and Team Spirit at Home.* Wheaton, Ill.: Victor, 1991.

Smalley, Gary, and John Trent. *The Blessing.* Nashville: Nelson, 1986.

Smith, Nathan. *Kidsport: A Survival Guide for Parents.* Reading, Mass.: Addison-Wesley, 1983.

Varni, James, and Donna Corwin. *Growing Up Great: Positive Solutions to Raising Confident, Self-Assured Children.* New York: Berkley Books, 1993.

RECOMMENDED VIDEOS

(Parents, preview them first, to make sure they're appropriate for your kids!)

Rudy

Fear Strikes Out!

A League of Their Own

Field of Dreams

The Karate Kid

Chariots of Fire

Angels in the Outfield

NATIONAL SPORT AND RECREATION ORGANIZATIONS

American Alliance for Health, Physical Education, Recreation and Dance
1900 Association Drive
Reston, VA 20191
703-476-3400 or 800-213-7193

American Sport Education Program
P.O. Box 5076
Champaign, IL 61825
800-747-4457
www.humankinetics.com

Boys and Girls Clubs of America
1230 W. Peach Street, N.W.
Atlanta, GA 30309
www.bgca.org

Disabled Sports USA
451 Hungerford Dr., #100
Rockville, MD 20850
301-217-0960

National Alliance for Youth Sports
2050 Vista Parkway
West Palm Beach, FL 33411
561-684-1141
www.nays.org

National Association of Police Athletic
    Leagues
618 North U.S. Highway 1, Suite 201
North Palm Beach, FL 33408
407-844-1823

Sport Information Resource Centre
107-1600 James Naismith Dr.
Gloucester, Ontario
    K1B 5N4 Canada
800-665-6413
www.sirc.ca
www.sportquest.com

YMCA
101 North Wacker Drive
Chicago, IL 60606
312-977-0031

YWCA
Empire State Building, #301
350 Fifth Avenue
New York, NY 10118
212-273-7800

Youth Sports Institute
IM Sports Circle
Michigan State University
East Lansing, MI 48824
517-353-6689

ORGANIZATIONS FOR SPECIFIC SPORTS:

American Softball Association
2801 NE 50th Street
Oklahoma City, OK 73111
405-424-3855
www.softball.org

American Youth Soccer
    Organization
5403 W. 138th Street
Hawthorne, CA 90250
800-USA-AYSO
fax: 310-643-5310

Dixie Boys Baseball, Inc.
P.O. Box 1778
Marshall, TX 75671-1778
903-927-1845
www.dixieorg/boys

Little League Baseball
P.O. Box 3485
Williamsport, PA 17701
717-326-1921
fax: 717-326-1074
www.littleleague.org

Pop Warner Little Scholars, Inc.
516 Middletown Blvd., Suite C-100
Langhorne, PA 19047
215-752-2691
fax: 215-752-2879

USA Hockey
4965 N. 30th Street
Colorado Springs, CO 80919
719-599-5500 or 800-566-3288
www.usahockey.com

Notes

INTRODUCTION

1. Shane Murphy, *The Cheers and the Tears* (San Francisco: Jossey-Bass, 1999), 25.

CHAPTER ONE

1. Shelley Youngblut, ed., *The Quotable ESPN* (New York: Hyperion Press/ESPN Books, 1998), 27.
2. Noelle Oxenhandler, "Room to Grow," quoted in *Reader's Digest*, December 1999, 112-23.
3. Adapted from Murphy, *The Cheers and the Tears*, 19-20.
4. From a survey of the 2000 U.S. Olympic softball team players.
5. Tim Hansel, quoted in "Points to Ponder," *Reader's Digest*, December 1992.

CHAPTER TWO

1. Survey conducted by the Kaiser Family Foundation and reported by Donna Britt, in the *Orlando Sentinel*, November 23, 1999.
2. Adapted from an item in the "Clips" section of *New Man* magazine, November-December 1994.
3. Ira Berkow in the *New York Times*, quoted in *Reader's Digest*, April 1996.
4. Youngblut, *The Quotable ESPN*, 179.
5. *Up Close*, 1991.
6. *Up Close*, 1993.
7. *Sunday Conversation*, 1991.

CHAPTER THREE

1. Reprinted from *Becoming a Couple of Promise*. Copyright ©1999 by Kevin Leman. Used by permission of NavPress, Colorado Springs, CO. All rights reserved.

CHAPTER FOUR

1. Youngblut, *The Quotable ESPN,* 47.
2. Gary Wilde in *The Quiet Hour* (Colorado Springs, David C. Cook, forthcoming: June 2000.
3. Youngblut, *The Quotable ESPN,* 46.
4. Lorne A. Adrain, *The Most Important Thing I Know About the Spirit of Sport* (New York: Morrow, 1999), 56.
5. Gerald May, author of *The Awakened Heart* (San Francisco: Harper and Row, 1991), spoken in a retreat workshop sponsored by Shalem Institute, Washington, D.C., December 7, 1993.
6. The material in this section draws heavily upon Dr. Smith's theory as expounded in Antoinette Saunders and Bonnie Remsberg, *The Stress-Proof Child* (New York: Holt, Rinehart and Winston, 1984), 129-42.

CHAPTER FIVE

1. Adrain, *The Most Important Thing I Know,* 114.
2. Adrain, *The Most Important Thing I Know,* 32.
3. Adapted from Miles McPherson, *The Power of Believing in Your Child* (Minneapolis: Bethany, 1998), 120.

CHAPTER SIX

1. Gary Wilde, ed., *Bible Promises to Treasure: For Dad* (Nashville: Broadman and Holman, 1998), 28.
2. John C. Friel and Linda D. Friel, *The 7 Worst Things Parents Do* (Deerfield Beach, Fla.: Health Communications, 1999), 83.
3. Robert Holmes, quoted in Lloyd Cory, ed., *Quote, Unquote* (Wheaton, Ill.: Scripture Press, 1977).
4. Richard Foster, *Celebration of Discipline* (San Francisco: Harper and Row, 1978), 70.
5. Vincent Fortanasce, *Life Lessons from Little League: A Guide for Parents and Coaches* (New York: Doubleday, 1995), 42.
6. Pat Conroy, in Joanna Powell's *Things I Should Have Said to My Father* (New York: Avon Books, 1994), 59.

CHAPTER EIGHT

1. Story by Karen Testa, the Associated Press, appearing in the *Orlando Sentinel,* November 18, 1999.

2. Reprinted from *Guidelines for Children's Sports* (1979) with permission from the National Association for Sport and Physical Education (NASPE), 1900 Association Drive, Reston, VA 20191-1599.

3. Chart content from Vanessa Ochs, *Safe and Sound: Protecting Your Child in an Unpredictable World* (New York: Penguin, 1995), as it appears in Joseph Biuso and Brian Newman, *Receiving Love* (Colorado Springs: Victor Books, 1996), 200.

4. Leah Adler, quoted by Beverly Levitt, "Burning Onions with Leah Adler," in the *Chicago Tribune,* September 26, 1999.

5. D. Ross Campbell, *How to Really Love Your Child* (Wheaton, Ill.: Victor, 1980), 36ff.

6. Robert Hastings, *Trusting Enough to Parent* (Colorado Springs: Chariot Victor, 2000), 110.

CHAPTER NINE

1. Adapted from Stephanie Marston, *The Magic of Encouragement: Nurturing Your Child's Self-Esteem* (New York: Morrow, 1990), 149-51.

2. John Bradshaw, *Healing the Shame That Binds You* (Deerfield Beach, Fla.: Health Communications, Inc., 1988), 11–12.

3. Marilyn Moravec, *Balancing Your Priorities* (Elgin, Ill.: David C. Cook, 1989), 52.

4. Adapted from Stephanie Marston, *The Magic of Encouragement: Nurturing Your Child's Self-Esteem* (New York: Morrow, 1990), 135.

CHAPTER TEN

1. Youngblut, *The Quotable ESPN,* 95–107.

2. Adapted from Ronald Smith and Frank Smoll, *Way to Go, Coach: A Scientifically Proven Approach to Coaching Effectiveness* (Portola Valley, Calif.: Warde Publishers, 1996), 109.

3. Smith and Smoll, *Way to Go, Coach,* 125-27.

4. From Tribune Media Services, in the *Orlando Sentinel,* November 23, 1999.

About the Authors

Jim Sundberg spent twenty-two years in major league baseball, sixteen of those years as a player for the Texas Rangers, Kansas City Royals, Chicago Cubs, and Milwaukee Brewers. In 1985 he won the World Championship with the Royals and was voted "World Series Hero" by the Chicago Sports Writers. He is a six-time Gold Glove winner and a three-time American League All-Star catcher. In the last six years of his baseball career he was an award-winning broadcaster and color analyst for the Texas Rangers television network. The Texas Rangers made him the namesake and first recipient of the team's annual "Jim Sundberg Community Service Award" for outstanding work in the North Texas area. Sundberg is also the founder of Sports Training Systems, an organization dedicated to the "family sports experience," which publishes comprehensive training products for coaches, children who play youth sports, and their parents.

Janet Sundberg is a native of Illinois, where she and Jim were high school sweethearts. She received her undergraduate degree in psychology from the University of Texas at Arlington and is pursuing her masters in occupational development. Currently she freelances as an organizational health consultant. In addition, Janet serves as a study group leader for Bible Study Fellowship. Jim and Janet have been married almost thirty years and have three children, Aaron, Audra, and Briana, all of whom have played competitive sports.

jim speaks!

After sixteen years playing major league baseball, which included being a three-time All-Star and a six-time Gold Glove winner, Jim Sundberg is probably best remembered for his starring role in winning the 1985 World Series. Today, Jim is still in demand across North America as a motivational speaker and personal leadership coach.

Using his wit and humor, Jim blends business principles with baseball analogies to convey valuable insights in ways people can easily understand.

Consider these timely topics:

- **"Balancing Family and Work"**
- **"Three Seasons of Dynamic Teams"**
- **"Career Transitioning"**

Jim's wife, Janet, is an organizational health specialist and can be available to speak with him on any of these topics for an even more dynamic event!

Jim's charismatic energy and enthusiasm quickly engage his audience

Helping the Kansas City Royals win 1985's World Series gave Jim personal insight into what makes winning teams

"I wish he was still in uniform!"
—*George W. Bush*

FOR MORE INFORMATION VISIT www.sportstolife.com

sports camps

Young athletes living in north Texas will want to consider attending Jim Sundberg's **Sports to Life** training camps for baseball and softball players.

Held at the beginning of summer at The Parks at Texas Star in Euless, Texas (between Fort Worth and Dallas), Jim's camps feature plenty of sports instruction, interaction, and fun! Both Jim and his softball coordinator, U.S. Olympian Jennifer McFalls, are on site daily, overseeing their handpicked staffs of experienced coaches. Each day features hands-on training, practice, games, lunch, and sports-to-life talks from well-known athletes who personify a wholesome sports attitude. Daytimes only, no sleepovers, and parents need to provide proof of insurance. Our instructor-to-student ratio is no higher than one to ten, so you know the kids are receiving the attention and supervision they deserve! Camp registration is limited, so be sure to check our Web site for the next camp registration dates!

Check out details for this year's camp info and get your registration form at: www.sportstolife.com

NOTARIZED REGISTRATION APPLICATION AND PROOF OF INSURANCE REQUIRED. PAYMENT MUST BE RECEIVED IN FULL BEFORE PARTICIPATION. REGISTRATION OPEN TO BOYS AND GIRLS AGES 7-16 REGARDLESS OF RACE, RELIGION, OR ETHNICITY. REGISTRATION IS FIRST COME FIRST SERVED.